Getting to Know John's Gospel

A Fresh Look at Its Main Ideas

Robert A. Peterson

Presbyterian and Reformed Publishing Company

GREAT COMMISSION PUBLICATIONS

Manufactured in the United States of America.

Library of Congress Cataloging-in-Publication Data

Peterson, Robert A., 1948-
    Getting to know John's Gospel : a fresh look at its main ideas /
Robert A. Peterson.
      p. cm.
    Includes indexes.
    1. Bible. N.T. John—Criticism, interpretation, etc. I. Title.
BS2615.2.P48 1989
226'.506—dc19   89-3809
    ISBN 0-87552-370-6 (P&R)   CIP
    ISBN 0-934688-52-4 (GCP)

01 / 7 6 5 4

Getting to Know
John's Gospel

To the person
who first taught me
to love the Greek New Testament,
Professor Mae E. Stewart,
Philadelphia College of Bible

Contents

Foreword

The Christian man or woman in the pew needs scriptural teaching he or she can understand. Here from the pen of a teacher and pastor comes a valuable guide to the Gospel of John aimed at real people where they live. This book will be used for many years to help folks understand the central truths of John's Gospel.

The author writes in such a way that you will comprehend every word, gain new insight, and know John better when you have finished. Most of all, you will know Jesus better.

Adult Sunday school classes, home Bible study groups, and individual Christians who want to grow in knowledge and faith can thank Robert A. Peterson for writing this clear and solid work.

John P. Sartelle
Independent Presbyterian Church
Memphis, Tennessee

Acknowledgments

I want to express my appreciation to the following friends, who read the manuscript for this book and made suggestions: Mary Beates, Kenneth Bush, David Deem, John Koontz, Sherry Kull, Janet LaSpina, Glyn Mangum, David McNamee, Robert Newman, James Pakala, Mary Pat Peterson, Ralph Ritter, William Snellbaker, Delno Supplee, and Barbara Weller. I also thank Mary Pat Peterson and Todd Mangum for their help in preparing the indexes. For patiently helping me improve as a writer, I thank editor Thom Notaro.

Introduction

In the spring of 1987 *Christian Mission* magazine told the story of a Ugandan boy who was found living among the monkeys of the jungle. His parents had been killed by Idi Amin's men, and the youngster had hid in the wild for as long as five years, where he learned to survive with the animals. Eventually Ugandan soldiers discovered the boy and brought him to a Christian orphanage.

Although he appeared normal, except for large calluses below his knees, Robert at first made animal sounds and chewed on grass and stones. Gradually, however, he began adjusting to civilized life.

Imagine that you were Robert on the day he was found by the soldiers. Adjusting to your new world would have been a monumental task. Think of all the new things you would have encountered: clothes, electric lights, refrigerators, cars, buildings—the list would have seemed endless. Imagine learning to read and write, to sing, to eat with a fork and knife, to play organized sports. There would have been so much to learn about your new world.

In a similar way the Gospel of John presents a world of ideas radically different from our own. It speaks of "the one who comes from above" and who is "above all" (3:31). It tells of "living water" (4:10, 11; 7:38), "the bread of life" (6:35), and "the light of the world" (8:12; 9:5), and of "the Son of Man" being "lifted up from the earth" (12:32, 34). Such concepts are naturally unfamiliar to us.

Getting to Know John's Gospel has been written to help you become better adjusted to the new world of ideas in the Gospel of John. My prayer is that you will grow in your faith as you grow in your understanding of this part of God's Word.

1

Why John Wrote His Gospel

Have you ever played the party game in which everyone tries to identify objects that are passed from person to person? You feel a bit foolish as you struggle to figure out what the objects are. The worst part is that they look so familiar, and yet you can't imagine the *purpose* of the various things. Then the host enlightens you. "This is a honey-dipper, used for dipping honey out of a jar without spilling it." Or, "This is an orange peeler."

As we look at Scripture, we can become perplexed for the same reason—we're often unaware of the purposes of the books of the Bible. The first step in studying the Gospel of John is to know *why* it was written.

John, the fourth Gospel, has at least three purposes:

- to bring people to salvation
- to strengthen Christians
- to defend the faith

Let's look at these purposes in order to apply the message of John more faithfully to our lives.

Bringing People to Salvation

We don't have to guess at the major purpose of John's Gospel. The apostle himself tells us his reason for writing.

> Jesus did many other miraculous signs in the presence of his disciples, which are not recorded in this book. But these are written that you may believe that Jesus is the Christ, the Son of God, and that by believing you may have life in his name (John 20:30-31).

3

Let's study these important verses. Jesus performed many more miracles than are recorded in the fourth Gospel. His nine miraculous "signs" in the Gospel of John are the following:

- turning water into wine (chap. 2)
- healing a royal official's son (chap. 4)
- healing a lame man (chap. 5)
- feeding the five thousand (chap. 6)
- rescuing his disciples on the Sea of Galilee (chap. 6)
- healing a blind man (chap. 9)
- raising Lazarus from the dead (chap.11)
- raising himself from the dead (chap. 20)
- giving his disciples a miraculous catch of fish (chap. 21)

Although we will not examine the significance of each miracle until our fourth and fifth chapters, here we want to notice their purpose. John 20:31 tells us, "But these are written that you may *believe*. . . ." Christ's miracles are reported in order to generate faith in the reader. In fact, John puts such emphasis on believing, that he uses the word *believe* ninety-nine times in his Gospel.

Where are we to put our faith? This is an important question because faith in an unreliable person is worthless, even dangerous. Think of the unfortunate people who followed Jim Jones to Jonestown, Guyana, and committed mass suicide with him in 1978. Though they put great confidence in Jones as a religious leader, their misplaced confidence proved destructive. We must put our confidence in the only one we can trust for salvation—Jesus Christ.

John tells us what he wants us to believe about Jesus, "That Jesus is the Christ, the Son of God" (20:31). We must believe that Jesus is the Jewish Messiah (the Christ). For this reason in each of the first twelve chapters of John's Gospel Jesus is presented as the Christ, the promised deliverer who fulfills the Old Testament. Furthermore, we must also believe that Jesus is the Son of God, equal with God the Father. I will say more about Jesus' being the Christ and the Son of God in our eighth and ninth chapters. Here we note that the fourth Gospel reports Jesus' miracles so that its readers would believe in his messiahship and divine sonship.

People are to trust Jesus as Messiah and Son of God so "that by believing [they] may have life in his name." John's ultimate concern is that believing readers may gain eternal life! Such life is later defined as knowing the Father and the Son (17:3). Thus John wrote that all who believe in Jesus enter into a personal relationship with the Father and the Son.

A look at the preceding verses (20:24-29) helps us understand John 20:30-31. Thomas is absent when Jesus first appears to his gathered disciples (see 20:19-24). Even when they later tell Thomas that they have seen the risen Christ, he answers, "Unless I see the nail marks in his hands and put my finger where the nails were, and put my hand into his side, I will not believe it" (v. 25). A week later Jesus makes a special appearance to the doubting Thomas and invites him to touch him and believe that he has risen from the grave. "Stop doubting and believe," Jesus tells him (v. 27). Thomas exclaims in response, "My Lord and my God!" And Jesus goes on to pronounce future believers truly happy (v. 29). We thus see the primary purpose of the Gospel of John fulfilled when Thomas believes in Jesus as his Lord and God.

We may summarize the first and major purpose of John's Gospel as follows:

SIGNS⟶ FAITH⟶ JESUS THE CHRIST⟶ ETERNAL LIFE
THE SON OF GOD

Has that major purpose of the Gospel of John been fulfilled in your life? Have you put all of your confidence for salvation in Jesus Christ alone? If you have not trusted Christ as Savior, I pray that you will come to do so as we study John together.

Strengthening Christians

John also wrote his Gospel to build up God's people in their faith. Although chapters 2-12 are designed primarily to lead people to salvation, they also enable believers to grow spiritually. Moreover, the chief purpose of chapters 13-17 is to help Christians make spiritual progress. I will select three passages from these chapters to demonstrate that the fourth Gospel's purpose is to strengthen Christians.

Jesus Washes His Disciples' Feet (13:1-17)

Knowing he must shortly leave the world and return to his Father, Jesus is about to show his great love for his own by dying on the cross for them (13:1-2). Having decided to spend the last hours before his death with his disciples, he does something unheard of—he washes their feet! No teacher was to do that for his students. In fact, students were not even supposed to wash their teacher's feet. This humble task was reserved for a servant. Yet, Jesus gets up from the evening meal, takes off his outer garment, and wraps a towel around his waist. He then pours water into a basin and begins to wash his disciples' feet, drying them with the towel (13:4-5).

In their amazement the disciples are all but speechless. Simon Peter, however, speaks up. "Lord, are you going to wash my feet?" When Jesus tells Peter that he would later understand the significance of the footwashing, Peter protests, "No, you shall never wash my feet" (13:8). Then Jesus replies, "Unless I wash you, you have no part with me." With characteristic exuberance Peter blurts out, "Then, Lord, not just my feet but my hands and my head as well!" Again Jesus surprises his disciples. "A person who has had a bath needs only to wash his feet; his whole body is clean. And you are clean, though not every one of you" (13:8-10).

Our Lord is teaching his followers an important truth. Unsaved people need to trust Jesus as Savior to have their sins forgiven once and for all. Once they are saved from sin's penalty, however, they still need daily cleansing from its pollution. Since he already is a believer in Jesus, Peter does not need a bath. He and the others (except Judas, the betrayer) need only to have their feet washed—they need frequently to confess their sins and accept the Lord's forgiveness.

These words of Jesus apply to twentieth-century Christians as well. Many believers are frustrated because they do not deal with their sins in God's way. Perhaps you have heard the joke about the foolish man who bought a gasoline-powered chain saw but failed to heed the salesman's advice to read the instructions. The next day the man angrily returned the saw, complaining that he had labored all day and managed to cut down only one tree. "What's the problem?" asked the salesman as he proceeded to start the saw. At the sudden roar the startled man jumped back and exclaimed, "What's that noise!"

Christians who fail to follow God's instructions on dealing with daily sin are as foolish as the man with the power saw. We must often confess our sins to the Lord to be cleansed from their defilement and to enjoy ongoing fellowship with him.

By washing his disciples' feet Jesus also teaches them another lesson. When he finishes the footwashing, puts on his outer garment, and returns to his place, he says:

> Do you understand what I have done for you? You call me "Teacher" and "Lord" and rightly so, for that is what I am. Now that I, your Lord and Teacher, have washed your feet, you should also wash one another's feet. I have set you an example that you should do as I have done for you. I tell you the truth, no servant is greater than his master, nor is a messenger greater than the one who sent him. Now that you know these things, you will be blessed if you do them (13:12-17).

Jesus gives the eleven disciples an unforgettable example of humble service when he stoops down to wash their feet. By deed and word he teaches them that they too must humbly serve others and thereby find true joy. How we need to follow Jesus' example today!

I have two friends who know the joy of which Jesus spoke. Ed and Bill drive the elderly to church, clean the church building, and generally help in any way possible. They are not paid to do these things; they do them because they love the Lord and his people. God's work would be furthered if the world saw more Eds and Bills humbly serving in love. Do you stoop to "wash the feet" of other Christians? May God give us grace not to exalt ourselves above our Lord Jesus, who took the place of a servant.

"Greater Things Than These" (14:12-14)

Jesus also seeks to strengthen his disciples in John 14:12-14. They are confused and discouraged because he has told them he will be going back to his father (13:33, 36; 14:2). Therefore, Jesus encourages them by saying: "I tell you the truth, anyone who has faith in me will do what I have been doing. He will do even greater things than these, because I am going to the Father" (14:12).

How is it possible for Jesus' followers to do greater things than he has done? How could anyone ever do something greater than the unique Son of God? Jesus explains in verses 13-14: "And I will do whatever you ask in my name, so that the Son may bring glory to the Father. You may ask me for anything in my name, and I will do it." After his death, burial, and resurrection Jesus will return to heaven, and he and the Father will answer believers' prayers. As a result of Jesus' earthly ministry of salvation prayers will be answered as never before! Praying in Jesus' name does not mean merely tacking the words "in Jesus' name" onto the end of a prayer. In fact, we do not find even one example of the apostles' doing this in the New Testament. Instead, to pray in Jesus' name means to pray with an awareness of the new access to God that we enjoy as a result of the work of the mediator, the Lord Jesus Christ.

An illustration helps clarify this idea. Since the Zimmerman family lived across from a playground, Mr. and Mrs. Zimmerman often supplied the equipment for the games their sons Charles and Craig played with their friends. When a neighborhood boy would simply ask to borrow equipment, the Zimmermans would turn him down. But if he would say, "Charles sent me to ask for the bats and balls," they would gladly grant the request. This is what it means for us to pray to God the Father in Jesus' name. We do not approach God on our own, but we come to the Father through Jesus our Savior.

I'll always remember a remarkable account of answered prayer told me by a friend.

As a city church in New Jersey grew in size, the congregation faced a shortage of parking facilities, which brought complaints from neighbors whose spaces were being taken by the cars of church-goers. Friends advised the church leaders to move to the suburbs where they could expand, but the leaders were committed to remaining in the city. Nonetheless, a hill on the church property prevented expansion where they were. So the pastor and other leaders brought their problem to God in prayer through his Son, Jesus.

Some time later a representative of the phone company called the pastor and explained that his company had done soil tests on various sites in the area. The tests showed that the type of dirt in the hill on the church's ground was precisely what the company needed for a project it had planned. To the pastor's amazement, the phone company agreed not only to remove the hill, but also to pay for the dirt. The thankful church now had the space for its new parking lot and enough money to pave it. The church's people had also received a lesson in how God answers believing prayers offered in Jesus' name.

When Jesus promises his disciples that they would do greater works than he, he does not mean works greater in *importance*. No one will ever do a more important work than Jesus' great work of dying and rising again to save us from our sins. Jesus means that in answer to prayer his followers will do works that are greater in *number* and more *widespread* than his. Jesus ministered in first-century Palestine to thousands of people; Argentine evangelist Luis Palau has ministered around the world to millions! Nevertheless, he recognizes that he is successful only because of Jesus' redemptive work and his promise in John 14:12-14.

God expects every believer in Christ to contribute to the "greater things" of which Jesus spoke. Each of us is to pray with the confidence that our Savior has opened to us a new access to God. And we are all to tell others of the love of God in sending his Son to be our deliverer. Perhaps God is calling you to be a missionary who will explain the message of salvation to people living in another culture.

The Vine and the Branches (15:1-17)

That John writes to strengthen his readers is also evident from Jesus' teaching concerning the vine and the branches in John 15. There Jesus applies to himself the Old Testament picture of Israel as the vineyard of the Lord (see, for example, Isa. 5:1-7). He, the true vine, takes the place of the disobedient nation that failed to accomplish its mission. Jesus' Father, the all-wise gardener, cuts off fruitless branches and prunes the fruit-bearing ones (15:2).

Does Jesus speak of two kinds of believers here, fruitful and fruitless Christians? No. People are either children of God or children of the devil (John 8:42-44). They either believe in the Son of God or do not (John 3:36). They either obey or disobey Christ's commandments (John 14:23-24). They either have eternal life or are spiritually dead (John 5:24). They either love the light or hate it (John 3:19-21). For John there are only two possibilities: either a person is a Christian or he is not. There is, therefore, no middle position between fruitfulness and fruitlessness.

The fruitless branch in John 15 is an unsaved person who has been "in the vine"—he has firsthand experience of the teachings and power of Jesus. In fact, the unfruitful branch that Jesus immediately has in mind is Judas. He has acted outwardly as a disciple should, appearing to be a fruitful branch, even fooling the other disciples (13:28-29). But in reality he is a fruitless one whose evil deeds will soon give him away. He has been a thief all along (12:4-6) and now has gone out to betray the Son of God (13:27, 30). Thus, one reason Jesus speaks of the vine and the branches is to prepare his disciples for Judas's treachery. The gardener will cut off the fruitless branches so that they can be gathered and thrown into the fire (John 15:2, 6). This is a picture of the eternal torment that Judas and those like him will suffer.

Jesus' threat of hell-fire is not directed at his disciples; he lets them know that he considers them fruitful branches. He uses a figure of speech in verses 2-3 (evident in the original Greek) called "paronomasia," which involves words with similar sounds but different meanings. Although the Father cuts off (Greek: *airei*) unfruitful branches, he cleans (*kathairei*) fruitful ones. Therefore, when Jesus tells his disciples that they are already clean (*katharoi*) because of the word he spoke to them, it is his way of assuring them that they are fruitful branches.

Moreover, Jesus is careful to speak of condemnation in 15:1-8 in the third person: "every branch in me that bears no fruit . . ." (v. 2) and "if anyone does not remain in me, he is like a branch . . ." (v. 6). In the surrounding verses, however, Jesus uses the second person to speak to the disciples: "You are already clean . . ." (v. 3); "apart from me you can do nothing" (v. 5); "if you remain in me . . ." (v. 7). Thus Jesus carefully distinguishes his disciples from the unfruitful branches that are headed for God's judgment.

John 15:8 sums up the main reason Jesus tells his disciples about the vine and the branches. "This is to my Father's glory, that you bear much fruit, showing yourselves to be my disciples." Since eternal life manifests itself in fruitfulness, the disciples are to prove that they are true believers by bearing fruit.

What does Jesus mean when he speaks repeatedly of "remaining" or "abiding" in the vine? He means remaining in his love (v. 9). Abiding is continuing in a personal relationship with Christ. Although Judas seems to have such a relationship with the Son of God, he really does not. The other disciples, however, are genuine fruit-bearing branches. They are to remain in the vine by continuing to love him who first loved them—Jesus. In so doing they will bear much fruit.

What kind of fruit is Jesus speaking about here? Some say he is talking about winning souls; others say the fruit of the Spirit. Although these would be included, the passage does not mention either one. Jesus is more general. The fruit of which he speaks is obedience to his commands (v. 10) and love for other believers (vv. 12-14). Moreover, Jesus himself is the disciples' model of both of these: he obeys his Father's commands (v. 10), and he gives the greatest example of love in laying down his life for them (vv. 12-13). Still another fruit is the great joy that comes from continuing in a warm personal relationship with Jesus (v. 11).

The disciples cannot take credit for bearing fruit. Ultimately they did not choose Jesus, but he chose them and appointed them to go and bear lasting fruit (v. 16). Since he chose them out of the world, they belong no longer to the world, but to him (v. 19).

Some time ago I had the privilege of sharing the gospel with a man I will call Antonio. After I told him that only Christ's death in our place can make us right with God, he seemed to understand. And yet I was unsure whether he trusted Christ as his Savior. My uncertainty grew as I lost contact with him for several months. Suddenly our paths crossed again, and I was surprised by what I saw. Antonio had obviously come to know the Lord—he was bearing much fruit by obeying the teachings of the Bible, praying for others, and sharing the gospel with his fellow workers. I was rebuked by the Lord for thinking that without my help Antonio would not become a Christian. God alone is the source of spiritual life. When he gave life to Antonio, that life expressed itself in fruit.

These three passages from John 13-15 demonstrate that these chapters are not primarily evangelistic; they do not present the way of salvation to an unsaved audience. Instead, the Savior is teaching his disciples what they would need to know after his death. The instructions of John 13-17 are intended to strengthen the disciples in their faith.

Defending the Christian Faith

The fourth Gospel presents a much different tone toward the Jews than does the Gospel of Matthew. Matthew reads as a tract for Jewish evangelism, while John seems almost hostile toward the Jews. Understanding John's frequent use of the phrase "the Jews" to mean the Jewish leaders opposed to Jesus does not really solve the problem; it just puts it in better focus. Why does the fourth Gospel speak so negatively about the Jewish leaders?

John writes his Gospel sometime during the last fifteen years of the first century, after the church's highly successful evangelizing of the Jewish people. By now the lines between the synagogue and church are tightly drawn. Gone forever are the days when the apostle Paul and others could witness for Jesus in a synagogue service.

At first glance the fourth Gospel's purpose of defending the faith may seem to run counter to its evangelistic purpose. John seeks to win Gentile converts to faith in Jesus, but what about Jews? Does he seek to convert "the enemy"? Understanding the historical situation at the time of the writing of the Gospel of John enables us to see that John does indeed seek to win Jews for Christ.

During the 80s of the first century the Jewish leaders tried to force Christian Jews out of the synagogues. That is dramatically illustrated for us in the chief prayer of the synagogues at the time, the Eighteen Benedictions. About the year 85 a curse on Jewish Christian "heretics" was added to the twelfth benediction. Since the Jews had to recite this prayer in the synagogue services, a Jewish Christian would thus be faced with a difficult choice: either curse himself or refuse to say the curse and thereby admit his belief in Jesus. Such an admission would result in his expulsion from the synagogue.

This background illumines for us the emphasis on confessing Christ in the fourth Gospel. John calls for Jews in his own day to believe in Christ and leave the synagogue. He does so by presenting to his readers three courageous Jewish believers: the blind man, Nicodemus, and Nathanael.

The Blind Man

The account of the blind man in John 9 is especially important. Jesus claims to be the light for the world and then gives sight to a blind beggar to prove it (9:5-7). The leaders of Israel, however, oppose Jesus and reject his light. In contrast, the blind man stands up for Jesus against "the Jews." Yet, when his parents are called in before the Pharisees, they refuse to discuss their son's healing "because they were afraid of the Jews, for already the Jews had decided that anyone who acknowledged that Jesus was the Christ would be put out of the synagogue" (9:22).

When the blind man attempts to lecture the Jewish authorities concerning the ways of God with man, and especially concerning Jesus, they excommunicate him in a rage (v. 34). Jesus, however, seeks the man out, who then believes in the Lord and worships him (vv. 35-38).

Christ gives a powerful concluding message (v. 39). He came into the world as its spiritual light, and his light both repels and attracts. It repels the Jewish leaders who refuse to see their spiritual blindness and thereby become hardened in their sins. It attracts the blind man who sees his spiritual need in Jesus' light and believes in him. The application to Jewish people still in the synagogue in John's day is plain: they must publicly confess their faith in Jesus even though it means excommunication.

Nicodemus

The three episodes where Nicodemus appears are also used to defend the Christian faith. In John 3 he comes to inquire of Jesus, who then instructs him concerning the new birth. Moreover, Jesus exposes Nicodemus's unbelief. "I have spoken to you of earthly things and you do not believe; how then will you believe if I speak of heavenly things?" (3:12).

We next find Nicodemus in chapter 7. The temple guards sent to arrest Jesus return to the Jewish leaders empty-handed. When the guards report amazement at Jesus' messages, the leaders are filled with anger.

> "You mean he has deceived you also?" the Pharisees retorted. "Has any of the rulers or of the Pharisees believed in him? No! But this mob that knows nothing of the law—there is a curse on them" (7:47-49).

Then Nicodemus questions the leaders whether they are following the guidelines of the law in their treatment of Jesus (7:50-51). John uses irony to make his point. The rulers have just accused the multitude of following Jesus because they are ignorant of the law. Now one of their own members points out that they are acting contrary to the law themselves. Nicodemus's response also indicates that at least one of the rulers and Pharisees (namely, Nicodemus) is willing to give Jesus a fair hearing—even if he himself has not yet believed in him.

In John 19 Nicodemus appears with Joseph of Arimathea, previously a secret disciple of Jesus (for fear of the Jews), who now has asked Pilate for Jesus' crucified body. To help Joseph prepare Jesus' body for burial, Nicodemus brings a mixture of costly spices, thus showing his love for the crucified Lord. The two men wrap Jesus' body and lay it to rest in a new garden tomb (19:39-42). Nicodemus thereby identifies himself with the accursed body of Jesus and publicly confesses him as Christ.

Nathanael

John's message is plain. The former blind man and Nicodemus

are examples of those who give up the synagogue to follow Jesus. John's Jewish readers should do the same. They should follow the example of Nathanael in 1:49 who confesses Jesus as the Son of God and King of Israel. Since Jesus proclaims him "a true Israelite in whom there is nothing false" (1:47), Nathanael stands in contrast to the Jewish leaders who are false Israelites, as John 8 shows. Although physically they are the descendants of Abraham, spiritually such leaders are children of their father, the devil (8:37-47).

Nathanael believes in Jesus the first time he meets him. In contrast to this true Israelite, "the Jews" are unmoved by Jesus' numerous signs and sermons. Even when Jesus raises Lazarus from the dead, their response is to issue a death warrant for Lazarus as they previously did for Jesus (12:10-11)!

We too can use the Gospel of John to defend the Christian faith. Many people are involved with cults that deny that Jesus is God. This is a serious error; if Jesus were not God he would not be able to rescue us from our sins. Since the fourth Gospel offers abundant testimony to Christ's deity, we need to study it so that we can help those ensnared by the cults.

Today many believers are afraid to confess Christ publicly for fear of persecution. The Gospel of John offers encouragement to us all to be like the blind man, Nicodemus, and Nathanael and to take a stand for the Lord Jesus, who loved us to the point of death.

As we have seen, the fourth Gospel has three primary purposes: to bring people to salvation, to strengthen Christians, and to defend the faith. Let us use this Gospel today by keeping in mind the purposes for which God gave it.

First, let us use John's Gospel to win the lost to Christ. I know of no better tool to use in an evangelistic Bible study than the fourth Gospel. I once led an outreach Bible study for more than a year on the Gospel of John. It was exciting to see people come to know Christ and his salvation. Perhaps you can consider opening your home for an evangelistic Bible study. Ask your pastor to supply the Bible teacher; you provide a friendly home and invite unsaved friends.

Second, let us use the Gospel of John to strengthen the people of

God. John's Gospel has been described as a river in which a child can wade and an elephant can swim. It presents the message of salvation as simply as anywhere in the Word of God, while also containing challenging teachings that make us think deeply to grasp their meaning. We will examine some of these more difficult ideas—John's doctrines of Christ, his saving work, the Holy Spirit, and the last things—in chapters 8-13 of this book. I invite you to strengthen your faith by opening the Gospel of John and thinking with me about these important topics.

Finally, let us use John's Gospel to defend the faith in our day. We need not be ashamed of believing in the Lord Jesus. Let us, therefore, commit ourselves to learning the teachings of John's Gospel well enough to be able to defend Christianity from attacks and to help those deceived by false teaching.

Review Questions

1. What are the three purposes of the Gospel of John?

2. Explain John 20:30-31 in your own words.

3. What two lessons did Jesus teach by washing his disciples' feet?

4. How could anyone ever do "greater things" than Jesus (John 14:12-14)?

5. Tell how Jesus' light both repels and attracts according to John 9.

Discussion Questions

1. What fruit (from John 15) do you need to cultivate in your life? Why don't we see more of this fruit in our lives?

2. Is daily confession of sin part of the normal Christian life? Is it an important part of your life? If not, what steps can you take to make it a more important part?

3. Name people in your fellowship who "wash the feet" of other believers. How can you be more like them?

4. Trace Nicodemus's pilgrimage to faith in the Gospel of John.

Compare it with Nathanael's response to Jesus. Do you know people whose conversion experience was like Nicodemus's? Like Nathanael's? What do we learn from studying their conversions?

5. In what specific ways can we today use John's Gospel in accordance with its divinely intended purposes?

2

How John's Gospel Is Put Together

"The difference between me and my mechanic," remarked Keith, "is that I know how to change a tire and check the oil, but he knows my car inside-out." Many of us are like my friend Keith. We know barely enough about our cars to get by. When we turn the key, the engine starts; when we flip a switch, the windshield wipers work. But woe unto us if the car doesn't start or the wipers don't work. That's when we wish we knew more of what a good mechanic knows—the way a car is put together.

Many Christians know their Bibles the way Keith knows his car. They know verses here and there, and a few portions of God's Word have special meaning to them. Yet they are unaware of the way the books of the Bible are put together. The Gospel of John especially contains many favorite verses and passages, but few people can describe its inner workings.

Studying the organization of the fourth Gospel will help us better understand its message so that we can apply it to our lives. John's basic outline is as follows:

- Introduction (chap. 1)
- Body (chaps. 2-20)
- Conclusion (chap. 21)

Chapter 1 introduces the Gospel, while chapters 2-20 make up its body. The conclusion, or epilogue, appears in chapter 21. Let us look in more detail at each of the three sections.

The Introduction (John 1)
The introduction divides neatly into two parts: 1:1-18 and 1:19-51.

The first part is the prologue, which speaks of the incarnation, the miracle that God became a man. Here John uses two word pictures to describe Jesus: he is the eternal Word of God and the true light. Jesus "the true light . . . was coming into the world" (1:9), which was spiritually dark, devoid of the knowledge of God. Coming into this dark world, the Son of God illuminated men and women with the message of salvation.

Furthermore, "the Word became flesh" (v. 14)—the eternal, almighty God became a man! The Son of God became something that he was not before—a flesh-and-blood human being. How fitting for John to begin this way, since Jesus' incarnation is the background for the rest of the Gospel. Being the God-man qualified him to do the miracles and proclaim the messages recorded in the remainder of the book.

If you were falsely accused of committing a crime and were taken to court, you would be grateful for those willing to testify on your behalf—your witnesses. Various figures appear as witnesses to Christ in the second part of the introduction: John the Baptist (vv. 19-36), Andrew (vv. 37-42), Philip, and Nathanael (vv. 43-51). Through them God testifies that Jesus is his Son and the Savior of the world. God's testimony to Jesus thus precedes the Jewish leaders' faulty estimation of him in chapters 2-12.

Here, then, is a sketch of John's introduction:

- Introduction
    1:1-18: Prologue (incarnation).
    1:19-51: Witnesses to Jesus.

The Body (John 2-20)

The body of the Gospel of John (2:1–20:31) subdivides into three sections: chapters 2-12, 13-17, and 18-20. The reasoning behind these subdivisions is worth considering. The introduction ends at the close of chapter 1. Chapter 2 begins with Jesus' first sign and initiates the large central section of the Gospel describing his public ministry (chaps. 2-12). In these chapters Christ performs miraculous signs and preaches sermons to the people, who respond in two ways. Some believe, but most reject him.

An important break occurs between chapters 12 and 13, and John appears to have four reasons for this division.

Reason 1: The Arrangement of the Signs

Although the first seven signs are clustered between chapters 2 and 11, there are no more signs until Jesus' resurrection in chapter 20. Thus the arrangement of these miraculous signs suggests a break somewhere after chapter 11 (I suggest after chapter 12).

Reason 2: The Distribution of the "Time" Sayings

The Gospel includes what are called "time" sayings to refer to Jesus' appointed time to die, rise again, and return to the Father. An example of such a saying occurs in 2:4 when Jesus tells his mother, "My time has not yet come." Although we will not investigate these sayings until our sixth chapter, here we note that the tense of the sayings suddenly changes in chapters 12 and 13. The "time" sayings mentioned in chapters 2-12 point to the future (Jesus' time has not yet come). However, starting with the end of chapter 12 (vv. 23, 27) and the beginning of chapter 13, Jesus' appointed time has arrived. To cite one example, John writes in 13:1, "Jesus knew that the time had come for him to leave this world and go to the Father." Thus as we plot the "time" sayings, chapters 2-12 (the time has not yet come) are distinguished from chapters 13 and following (the time has come).

Reason 3: The Shift in Audiences

Another reason for dividing the Gospel of John between chapters 12 and 13 is the shift of audiences in the book. In chapters 2-12 Jesus speaks primarily to the multitudes and Jewish leaders. However, in chapters 13-17 he speaks privately to his disciples.

Reason 4: A Comparison of 12:37 and 20:30-31

A comparison of 12:37 and 20:30-31 supports dividing the Gospel of John as I have suggested. John made these passages parallel so that we might set them side by side and discover the plan of his Gospel. John 12:37 reads,

> Even after Jesus had done all these miraculous signs in their presence, they still would not believe in him.

Compare that with 20:30-31:

> Jesus did many other miraculous signs in the presence of his disciples, which are not recorded in this book. But these are written that you may believe that Jesus is the Christ, the Son of God, and that by believing you may have life in his name.

Admittedly, these two passages have certain similarities. Both teach that Jesus performs sign-miracles and that he does the signs in the presence of others. But the similarities end there. Consider the different audiences. In chapter 12 Jesus does his miracles "in their presence"—in the presence of the unbelieving Jews. In 20:30, however, he does them "in the presence of his disciples."

The greatest difference between the two passages is the two divergent responses to Jesus' ministry. Although John 12:37 reports that "they still would not believe in him," John 20:31 tells us that the purpose of Jesus' ministry is that people might believe in him and gain eternal life. Therefore, John 12:37 summarizes the basic response of the Jews to Jesus in chapters 2-12—unbelief; John 20:30-31 sums up the response of the disciples—belief in Jesus. In fact, Thomas represents the others when he makes his confession of Jesus, "My Lord and my God!" (20:28). In our seventh chapter we will study the patterns of belief and unbelief in the Gospel of John.

Thus we have four reasons for dividing the Gospel of John between chapters 12 and 13.

Chapters 13-17 belong together because in them Jesus withdraws from the world and teaches his disciples alone. As a sailor leaving for a tour of sea duty prepares his children for his departure, so Jesus prepares his disciples for his return to the Father. He impresses upon them the importance of their loving one another. Knowing that difficult times lie ahead of his disciples, he teaches them what the Holy Spirit will do in their lives. Moreover, because of Jesus' coming death, resurrection, and ascension, his followers will enjoy a new access to God in prayer. In addition, Jesus promises to return to take them to be with him in heaven.

Chapters 18-20 form a unit because of their historical subject matter. Jesus' arrest, his appearances before Annas, Caiaphas, and Pilate, and Peter's denials are all reported in chapter 18. Chapter 19 includes Jesus' sentencing, crucifixion, death, and burial. We learn of his resurrection and appearances to Mary of Magdala, his disciples, and Thomas in chapter 20.

Here is our outline of John, chapters 2-20.

- Body
  2-12: Jesus' signs and sermons, met with Jewish disbelief.
  13-17: Jesus teaches his disciples privately.
  18-20: Jesus' arrest, trials; Peter's denials; Jesus' crucifixion, death, and resurrection.

The Conclusion (John 21)

The Gospel of John concludes with an epilogue that records the ninth sign—the miraculous catch of fish on the Sea of Galilee (21:1-14). The major purpose of this section is to show the disciples the importance of the church's missionary task. Without Jesus they fish all night and catch nothing; at his word their nets are bursting with big fish. Similarly, if they trust in their own efforts alone in evangelism, they will "catch" nothing. But if they trust him who promised to make them "fishers of men," they will lead many to Jesus.

John 21:15-25, the second part of the epilogue, describes Jesus' reinstatement of Peter and teaches the importance of the discipling ministry of the church. Peter and the others are to "feed Jesus' sheep" by instructing them in the Word and ways of God. Thus the Gospel ends by focusing the disciples' attention and ours on the two most important tasks of the church—evangelism and discipleship.

Our analysis of the structure of the fourth Gospel can be outlined as follows:

- Introduction
  1:1-18: Prologue (incarnation).

1:19-51: Witnesses to Jesus.
- Body
    2-12: Jesus' signs and sermons, met with Jewish unbelief.
    13-17: Jesus teaches his disciples privately.
    18-20: Jesus' arrest, trials; Peter's denials; Jesus' crucifixion, death, and resurrection.
- Conclusion
    21:1-14: The miraculous catch of fish.
    21:15-25: Jesus reinstates Peter.

Prompted by her pastor's sermons, Mary faithfully read her Bible for years. She especially grew to love certain passages in the Gospel of John and even taught a women's Bible study on it. After learning the outline of the fourth Gospel presented here, she understood her favorite passages for the first time in the context of the whole book. Other passages that previously had seemed obscure now opened up to her. Mary saw how the parts of the Gospel fit together to form a whole. Since she now had a road map enabling her to find her way around in the Gospel of John, she gained confidence in sharing its message with others. It is my prayer that Mary's experience may be yours also.

Review Questions

1. List the witnesses to Jesus in John 1:19-51.

2. Review the four reasons for dividing the Gospel of John between chapters 12 and 13.

3. Compare and contrast John 12:37 with 20:30-31.

4. What are some of the topics Jesus covers in chapters 13-17?

5. Summarize the outline of the Gospel of John. Can you write it out from memory?

Discussion Questions

1. Tell how John uses the pictures of Word and light to describe the incarnation in the prologue.

2. What do each of the witnesses in John 1:19-51 say about Jesus?

3. Tell how John 21 can strengthen our evangelism and discipleship.

4. How does studying the organization of John's Gospel help you better understand it?

5. How does your knowledge of the outline of John help you explain verses 6:66 and 16:33?

3

Jesus' "I Am" Sayings

Some people are easier to get to know than others. I studied under two outstanding professors of church history in graduate school. Both were capable scholars and fine Christian men. Both excelled in their respective teaching styles. Professor J was best one on one; Professor B was a master in the classroom. Their personalities were as distinct as their styles of teaching. Since Professor J was approachable and his office was open to students, I got to know him almost immediately. Professor B was more reserved, and, although I wanted very much to become his friend, it took me two years to do so.

Jesus freely makes himself known to his disciples. In the Gospel of John he does so by means of his "I am" sayings. These are sayings in which Jesus says "I am the. . . ," followed by some description of his role. Examples of his "I am" sayings are "I am the good shepherd" (10:11) and "I am the resurrection and the life" (11:25). Not included among these "I am" sayings are cases where Jesus says simply, "I . . . am he" (as in 4:26). Also excluded is Jesus' important statement, "Before Abraham was born, I am" (8:58) because it does not fit the pattern of "I am the. . . ."

Below are the seven "I am" sayings in the Gospel of John:

- "I am the bread of life" (6:35, 48, 51).
- "I am the light of the world" (8:12; 9:5).
- "I am the gate" (10:7, 9).
- "I am the good shepherd" (10:11, 14).
- "I am the resurrection and the life" (11:25).
- "I am the way and the truth and the life" (14:6).
- "I am the true vine" (15:1, 5).

The "I am" sayings, like many of John's ideas, are rooted in the

Old Testament. Their Old Testament background is the announcement of the prophets who spoke for God and said, "Thus says the Lord." Jesus acts as a prophet, a spokesman for God, when he says, "I am the. . . ." In fact, Jesus is more than a prophet; he himself is revelation from God. The Father sent the Son into the world to reveal God. Thus when Jesus says, "I am the way and the truth and the life," he is explaining God to his disciples.

Jesus says "I am" instead of "Thus says the Lord" because he is claiming to reveal God directly in a way that other prophets could not. Elijah, Isaiah, Jeremiah, and Ezekiel were spokesmen for God. With hands extended toward heaven, they announced, "Thus says the Lord." But Jesus, having come from heaven, says, "I am the light of the world." Therefore, when Jesus speaks for God in the first person, he is claiming to be God himself.

Jesus' "I am" sayings are also similar to the words of the Lord in the latter chapters of Isaiah. Isaiah 43:11-12 is a good example: "I, even I, am the Lord, and apart from me there is no savior. I have revealed and saved and proclaimed. . . ." If Jesus is referring to passages such as this when he says "I am the . . . ," then he is claiming to be the Lord of the Old Testament.

Although there are seven "I am" sayings, they have only three different meanings: Jesus is the revealer of God, the Savior, and the giver of eternal life. He summarizes these three in 14:6 where he says, "I am the way and the truth and the life." We can arrange the "I am" sayings of Jesus in the fourth Gospel using these three meanings as an outline.

- Jesus is the revealer of God.
  "I am the truth."
  "I am the light of the world."
- Jesus is the Savior.
  "I am the way."
  "I am the gate."
- Jesus is the giver of eternal life.
  "I am the life."
  "I am the bread of life."
  "I am the good shepherd."

"I am the resurrection and the life."
"I am the true vine."

Jesus Is the Revealer of God

"I Am the Truth"

When Jesus says "I am the truth" (14:6), he means that he came from heaven to bring God's truth to the world. A few verses later he says, "The words I say to you are not just my own. Rather, it is the Father, living in me, who is doing his work" (v. 10). Since Jesus speaks the Father's words, knowing Jesus is knowing the Father. Amazingly, seeing Jesus is seeing the Father (vv. 7, 9)! Jesus is the revealer of the invisible God.

Jesus also speaks to Pilate about the truth. "In fact, for this reason I was born, and for this I came into the world, to testify to the truth" (18:37). Jesus not only bears the truth—according to 14:6 he *is* the truth; he himself is revelation from God.

Jesus' status as the revealer of God should influence our reading of the Gospels. As we read Matthew, Mark, Luke, or John, we tend to regard Jesus merely as a good example. Frankly, we often don't know how else to look at him. However, Jesus' statement "I am the truth" tells us that Jesus is more than a role model. Since Jesus is the revealer of God, whenever Jesus performs an action or speaks, he teaches us about God. So when we read of Jesus gathering the children to himself (Matt 19:13-15), we learn about the way God acts. When we read Jesus' Sermon on the Mount (Matt. 5-7), we learn about the way God speaks. Since Jesus is the revealer of God, we must read the deeds and words of Jesus recorded in the Gospels as the revealed truth about God.

"I Am the Light of the World"

Christ's saying "I am the light of the world" has the same meaning as "I am the truth."

Bright lights shone in the temple in the Court of the Women

during the Feast of Tabernacles in Jerusalem. At the end of the feast the lights were extinguished. Against this background of darkness Jesus claims, "I am the light of the world" (John 8:12).

When Jesus repeats this "I am" saying in 9:5, he backs up his claim by healing a man born blind (9:6-7). By performing the physical miracle he demonstrates that he has the ability to grant spiritual sight. Later the blind man comes to believe in Jesus, the light of the world (v. 38). By contrast, the Pharisees refuse to see by Jesus' light; they claim that they understand spiritual things apart from him and his revelation from God. As a result Jesus' light blinds them, and they remain in their sins (vv. 39-41; see pp. 37-39).

Philip P. Bliss's well-known gospel song captures the sentiments of believing hearts.

> The whole world was lost in the darkness of sin;
>   The Light of the world is Jesus;
> Like sunshine at noonday His glory shone in;
>   The Light of the world is Jesus.

[Refrain]

> Come to the Light, 'tis shining for thee;
>   Sweetly the light has dawned upon me;
> Once I was blind, but now I can see;
>   The Light of the world is Jesus.

Many people today testify that Jesus is indeed the light in their lives. Although Frank, for instance, had been attending a Bible-believing church for a year, he had not become a Christian. One Sunday morning he felt that the preacher was talking right to him. Frank bowed his head and quietly thanked God that Jesus died to save him from the penalty of his sins. When asked why he trusted Christ on that particular day, Frank replied, "All of a sudden God turned the lights on in my mind." That was Frank's way of saying that Jesus, the light of the world, had illuminated him.

Jesus Is the Savior

"I Am the Way"

Jesus is "the way." No one comes to the Father except through him (14:6). Referring to heaven as God's house with many rooms, Jesus announces that he is returning there to prepare a place for his disciples. In addition, he promises to come back to take them to be with him (vv. 2-3). Obviously, each disciple is precious to God. Each belongs to the Father and is welcome in his presence in heaven. Jesus' words have comforted many Christians, and they still comfort believers today by assuring us that our Savior will one day return to take us into the Father's presence.

Although Jesus says that the disciples know the way to the Father's house, Thomas admits that they do not know where Jesus is going or the way there (vv. 4-5). Thus Jesus says, " I am the way. . . . No one comes to the Father except through me." The modern idea of heaven as a big city with many highways leading into it is false. There is but one way to the Father's house. Jesus is the only road that leads to heaven.

"I Am the Gate"

Christ's words "I am the gate" (10:7, 9) have the same meaning as "I am the way," with one small difference. Here Jesus is speaking not of the Father's house in heaven, but of the shepherd and his sheep on earth. The sheep represent the true people of God, and Jesus is their shepherd who cares for them. By contrast, the Pharisees are the thieves and robbers who want to harm the sheep. Inasmuch as God's people believe in Jesus ("listen to his voice") and obey ("follow") him, they reject the false shepherds, the Pharisees (10:1-6).

We must read John 10 with the preceding chapter in mind. The blind man healed by Jesus is a sheep who follows the Lord and refuses to listen to the Pharisees (9:25, 30-33, 35-38). Conversely, the leaders of Israel are false shepherds who put the former blind man out of the synagogue for believing in Christ (9:34).

In that context Jesus claims, "I am the gate for the sheep. All who ever came before me were thieves and robbers, but the sheep did not listen to them. I am the gate; whoever enters through me will be saved" (10:7-9). Since Jesus is the only door into the sheepfold of the true people of God, he is the only way to salvation.

I confess that I was a churchgoer for some years before I believed in Jesus, the Savior of the world, as *my* Savior. I am thankful that the Lord Jesus overcame the pull of the world in my life and drew me to himself. If you have not done so, why not trust the Good Shepherd to bring you into the fold right now?

Perhaps W. Spencer Walton's hymn will speak to your heart as it does to mine.

> In tenderness He sought me,
>   Weary and sick with sin,
> And on His shoulders brought me,
>   Back to His fold again.
> While angels in His presence sang
> Until the courts of heaven rang.
>
> He washed the bleeding sin-wounds,
>   And poured in oil and wine;
> He whispered to assure me,
>   "I've found thee, thou art Mine";
> I never heard a sweeter voice;
> It made my aching heart rejoice!
>
> He pointed to the nail-prints,
>   For me His blood was shed,
> A mocking crown so thorny
>   Was placed upon his head:
> I wondered what He saw in me,
> To suffer such deep agony.
>
> I'm sitting in His presence,
>   The sunshine of His face,
> While with adoring wonder,
>   His blessings I retrace.
> It seems as if eternal days
> Are far too short to sing His praise.

[Refrain]

Oh, the love that sought me!
Oh, the blood that bought me!
Oh, the grace that brought me to the fold,
Wondrous grace that brought me to the fold.

Jesus Is the Giver of Eternal Life

"I Am the Life"

We have seen that Jesus is *the truth*, the revealer of God, and as revealer he makes known that he is *the way* to God, the Savior. How then does Jesus save us? He does so by giving us spiritual life because he is *the life*—the giver of eternal life.

"I Am the Bread of Life"

Realizing that bread was the basic food in first-century Palestine gives us insight into Jesus' feeding the five thousand in John 6:1-14. By multiplying the loaves (and the fish) Jesus provides the people with what was necessary for life. He then gives the message, "I am the bread of life" (6:35). Jesus communicates forcefully by combining the miracle and the "I am" saying. As the loaves of bread gave physical life to those who ate them, so he gives eternal life to all who believe in him.

"I Am the Good Shepherd"

Jesus the Good Shepherd lays down his life for his sheep (10:11). In fact, since he loves them so much, he voluntarily dies on their behalf. And yet Jesus' death is not a defeat, because he triumphs over death when he lays down his life and takes it up again (vv. 17-18).

Because Jesus died and rose again, he is able to give eternal life to his sheep. "I give them eternal life," he says, "and they shall never perish; no one can snatch them out of my hand. My Father, who has given them to me, is greater than all; no one can snatch them out of my Father's hand" (10:28-29). Eternal life is a gift from Jesus, the Good Shepherd, who guarantees that his sheep will never perish. They are safe because he and the Father hold them in their hands. Therefore, when Jesus says "I and the Father are one" (v. 30), he means that he and the Father are one in their ability to keep the people of God safe.

My friend Ken once told me, "I struggled in my early Christian experience because I lacked the assurance of salvation. Without that good foundation nothing in my life worked the way it was supposed to. I wanted to grow, but was hindered." Ken was overjoyed when someone taught him from the Scriptures that God the Son had given him eternal life. His life was revolutionized when he understood that the Father and the Son would keep him safe forever.

Ken has since grown into a mature believer who actively serves the Lord. Nevertheless, he has not forgotten the importance of a good beginning. After he leads someone to Christ, he trains him or her in the basics of Christian living. "I try to help others get a better start than I had," Ken says. "And that includes teaching them the importance of the assurance of salvation."

"I Am the Resurrection and the Life"

Surprisingly, after Mary and Martha send word that their brother Lazarus is very ill (11:1-3), Jesus delays before going to see him (vv. 6, 14-15). When Jesus finally comes to Bethany, Martha goes out to meet him. She tells him that if he had been there, her brother would not have died. In reply Jesus tells her that Lazarus will rise again.

"I know he will rise again in the resurrection at the last day," says Martha (vv. 23-24). The Old Testament had predicted the resurrection of the dead (Dan. 12:2). But Jesus goes a step further: "I am the resurrection and the life. He who believes in me will live, even though he dies; and whoever lives and believes in me will never die. Do you believe this?"

"Yes, Lord," she tells him, "I believe that you are the Christ, the Son of God, who was to come into the world" (11:25-27). John gives us an illustration of his main purpose—to lead people to salvation—

as Martha confesses Jesus as Christ and Son of God (see 20:30-31 and pp. 3-5).

After Martha's sister Mary meets Jesus, he goes to the tomb. There he raises the dead man from the grave by shouting, "Lazarus, come out!" (11:43). By word and deed Jesus reveals that he is the giver of eternal life. Raising Lazarus physically is an example of Jesus' ability to make the spiritually dead come alive.

Imagine yourself standing outside of Lazarus's tomb and calling him to come forth. What would happen? You might yell yourself hoarse, but you could never raise him from the dead. Nevertheless, we sometimes act as if we are able to give another person eternal life. How foolish! We need to recognize our complete dependence upon the Lord Jesus, who alone gives eternal life to those who are spiritually dead.

"I Am the True Vine"

"I am the true vine," Jesus says to his disciples (15:1). Just as a vine gives life to its branches, so Jesus gives spiritual life to his true disciples. True believers produce fruit because of their connection with the vine (15:2-5). False believers, however, are fruitless because they have no vital link to the Lord Jesus Christ, the source of eternal life (vv. 2, 6).

Here then are the meanings of Jesus' seven "I am" sayings in the Gospel of John:

"I Am" Saying and Reference	*Meaning:* Jesus Is the...
• "I am the bread of life" (6:35, 48, 51).	giver of eternal life
• "I am the light of the world" (8:12; 9:5).	revealer of God
• "I am the gate" (10:7, 9).	Savior
• "I am the good shepherd" (10:11, 14).	giver of eternal life
• "I am the resurrection and the life" (11:25).	giver of eternal life
• "I am the way	Savior
and the truth	revealer of God
and the life" (14:6).	giver of eternal life
• "I am the true vine" (15:1, 5).	giver of eternal life

We have all known people who were reluctant to visit a doctor because they didn't want to face the seriousness of their illnesses. Similarly, many of us avoid spiritual things because we are afraid to acknowledge our condition before God. Speaking of Jesus as the light, the fourth Gospel says: "Light has come into the world, but men loved darkness instead of light because their deeds were evil. Everyone who does evil hates the light, and will not come to the light for fear that his deeds will be exposed" (3:19-20).

We cannot hide our sins from God, for he knows them better than we do. Admittedly, to face up to our sins is painful, yet it is the first step toward the kingdom of God. Only when we see our own sinfulness can we trust Jesus as Savior. Come to the light. Ask God for mercy—and believe that Jesus died and rose again to save you from your sins. Receive eternal life as a gift from Jesus, the only one who can give it to you.

Review Questions

1. Explain in what ways Jesus is more than a prophet.

2. Tell how John 14:6 summarizes the three different meanings of the "I am" sayings.

3. Mark each of the following "I am" sayings with its meaning (R= Revealer of God, G= Giver of eternal life, S= Savior):

    _____ Bread of life   _____ Gate

    _____ Good shepherd   _____ Resurrection and life

    _____ True vine   _____ Light of the world

4. What does Jesus communicate in John 9 by his "I am" saying and miracle? Explain.

5. Tell how Jesus' being the way to the Father's house and the gate into the sheepfold teach that he is the Savior.

Discussion Questions

1. Why doesn't Jesus say "Thus says the Lord" in John?

2. Why should Jesus' being the revealer of God help us get more out of our reading of the Gospels?

3. Why is Jesus' combination of word ("I am the bread of life")

and deed (the feeding of the five thousand) more effective than either one alone?

4. How do the words of Jesus, the "good shepherd" in John 10, give us assurance of salvation?

5. In what ways should the fact that Jesus is the giver of eternal life strengthen our evangelism?

4

Jesus' Miraculous "Signs" (1)

Everyone in the rural church knew that the Collins family was having a difficult time. Being very concerned, the congregation called a special meeting to talk about how they could help. As the meeting was about to begin, the people buzzed about the conspicuous absence of Seth Rogers, an elderly single man who rarely missed a church meeting. How humbled they were the next day to learn what Seth had been doing while they were meeting for discussion. After loading up his station wagon with food and other necessities, he had driven over to the Collins place. As old Seth put it, "There is a time for talkin' and a time for doin', and this was a time for doin'."

Jesus is both a talker and a doer in the Gospel of John. He not only preaches, but also performs nine "signs" or miracles.

- Jesus turns water into wine at the wedding in Cana (2:1-11).
- Jesus heals the royal official's son in Galilee (4:46-54).
- Jesus heals a lame man by the pool of Bethesda in Jerusalem (5:1-15).
- Jesus feeds the five thousand by multiplying the loaves and fish in Galilee (6:1-15).
- Jesus rescues his disciples on the Sea of Galilee (6:16-21).
- Jesus heals a man born blind (9:1-41).
- Jesus raises Lazarus from the grave in Bethany (11:1-44).
- Jesus raises himself from the dead (20:1-29).
- Jesus gives the disciples a miraculous catch of fish on the Sea of Galilee (21:1-14).

Often in the Scriptures God makes himself known both by word and by deed. This holds true for the ministry of Jesus in the fourth

Gospel. In both word (the "I am" sayings and sermons) and deed (the signs) Jesus makes God the Father known. In fact, the signs communicate the same things about Jesus (and the Father) as the "I am" sayings. Therefore, I will use essentially the same three major headings to discuss the signs as I used for the "I am" sayings in the previous chapter: Jesus, the revealer of God; Jesus, the giver of eternal life; and Jesus, the Savior. We will look at the first two headings in this chapter and the third in the next.

Jesus, the Revealer of God

Jesus Heals a Man Born Blind (9:1-41)

For years missionaries Bill and June Ghrist operated an eye clinic in Kenya, East Africa. Bill performed hundred of operations to improve people's sight. Because the Ghrists loved the Kenyans, they were delighted to use medicine to help show them Jesus' love. In so doing they followed Jesus' example of treating people's physical sight in order to help them to see spiritually.

Jesus heals the blind man to demonstrate that he is the revealer of God. By combining this sign with his saying "I am the light of the world," Jesus proves that he is the spiritual illuminator.

The plight of a blind man in first-century Palestine was pitiable. Not being able to obtain an education, he more than likely had to beg for food. To exemplify man's need for mercy, blind beggars appear here (9:8) and elsewhere in the Gospels (Mark 10:46 and Luke 18:35).

Evidently, the disciples and Pharisees believe a myth—that the man's blindness is a punishment for sins committed in his mother's womb or for his parents' sins (see 9:2, 34). Jesus, however, disagrees. "Neither this man nor his parents sinned, but this happened so that the work of God might be displayed in his life" (v. 3).

After spitting on the ground, Jesus makes mud with the saliva. Having applied the mud to the blind man's eyes, he tells him to go wash in the pool of Siloam. The blind man obeys and gains his sight. Since the man's neighbors are confused over whether he is the man born blind, he assures them that he is indeed the man Jesus healed

(vv. 6-9). There may well be a touch of humor in his insistence, "I am the man" (v. 9).

Contrasting the Pharisees and the blind man, John 9 records Jesus' granting sight to the poor, uneducated man. As the man grows in his understanding of Jesus, so his response to Jesus deepens. He first calls him "the man they call Jesus" (v. 11); next, "a prophet" (v. 17); and then, "this man . . . from God" (v. 33). Finally, the blind man believes in Jesus and worships him (v. 38). The Jewish leaders, however, respond to Christ much differently. Instead of growing in their understanding of Jesus, they oppose him more and more bitterly. First they interrogate the formerly blind man (vv. 13-17), then his parents (vv. 18-23), and then him again (vv. 24-34) as they resist the meaning of this miraculous sign.

John writes here with irony and sarcasm. An uneducated blind man knows more about God than the religious leaders of Israel! When Jesus, the light of the world, shines on the blind man, he confesses: "Nobody has ever heard of opening the eyes of a man born blind. If this man were not from God, he could do nothing" (vv. 32-33). Admittedly, Jesus' light shines on the Pharisees, too, but they reject him and harden their hearts. Unwilling to accept the man's testimony about Christ, they excommunicate him from the synagogue.

We can now understand Jesus' puzzling words at the end of chapter 9: "For judgment I have come into this world, so that the blind will see and those who see will become blind" (v. 39). As Jesus the revealer shines on people with the knowledge of God, he brings about a radical separation. The "blind" who recognize their spiritual blindness in his light will gain spiritual sight ("see"). But those who claim that they have spiritual wisdom apart from him ("those who see") will be confirmed in their unbelief ("will become blind").

John 9:40-41 confirms this interpretation. Some Pharisees who are with Jesus ask scornfully: "What? Are we blind too?" Because they assume that they are full of wisdom from God, their question really means, We are not spiritually ignorant, are we? However, Jesus has just used the word "blind" in a different sense—to mean "spiritually needy." Jesus, therefore, answers them, "If you were blind [if you saw your spiritual need], you would not be guilty of sin [you would believe in me and I would forgive your sins]; but now that you claim you can see [you claim to have spiritual wisdom apart from me, the light of the world], your guilt remains [I will not forgive you as long as you reject me]" (v. 41).

As a monk Martin Luther went to great lengths trying to earn God's favor. When told that confession of sins was the way to God, Luther tried to confess every sin he had ever committed. Ransacking his memory back to childhood, he confessed his sins so zealously that his exasperated confessor protested, "Look here, if you expect Christ to forgive you, come in with something to forgive—murder, blasphemy, adultery—instead of all these little nothings."

Believing that prayer and fasting opened the door to heaven, Luther prayed and fasted so much that he damaged his health. Thinking the abuse of his body pleased God, Luther beat himself often to tame his evil nature.

When Luther later looked back on these attempts to merit salvation, he exclaimed, "If ever a monk could be saved by his monkery, I was the man!" Yet he wasn't the man; all his attempts failed to give him assurance of acceptance with God. Mercifully, Luther's superior, John Staupitz, fearing that Martin would kill himself if he continued his present course, directed him to study the Bible.

Jesus Christ, the revealer of God, enlightened Luther as he pored over the pages of Paul's Epistle to the Romans. Luther came to understand from Romans 1:17 that God declares sinners righteous when they believe in Jesus. At last Luther received the assurance of salvation he had craved so long. That assurance came not from his efforts to earn God's favor, but from trusting Jesus, who died for him and rose again. Overwhelmed with God's grace, Luther thanked God that Jesus opens the eyes of the blind.

Could it be that someone reading this chapter is trying, as Luther did, to win God's favor? If so, you don't need to repeat Luther's struggles. Turn from all your efforts of self-salvation and ask Jesus, the revealer of God, to illumine you as you read the Gospel of John. Ask him to give you the confidence that he is able to save you from your sins by his death and resurrection.

Jesus, the Giver of Eternal Life

Five of the signs show Jesus to be the giver of eternal life.

Jesus Heals the Royal Official's Son (4:46-54)

The son of a royal official is near death. Jesus tells the concerned father: "You may go. Your son will live" (4:50). Taking Jesus at his word, the man heads home. On the way, his servants bring the news that his son has gotten better. When the royal official finds out that the recovery occurred at the very hour that Jesus told him, "Your son will live," he and his family believe in Christ (vv. 51-53). By giving physical life to a boy near death, Jesus demonstrates that he has the ability to give eternal life.

Jesus Heals a Lame Man by the Pool of Bethesda (5:1-15)

At the pool of Bethesda in Jerusalem Jesus heals a man who has been lame for thirty-eight years by saying: "Get up! Pick up your mat and walk." At once the man is cured (5:8-9). Here again by using a physical healing John proves that Jesus is able to give spiritual life. Moreover, Jesus' sermon following the miracle confirms that he is the life-giver. "For just as the Father raises the dead and gives them life," Jesus preaches, "even so the Son gives life to whom he is pleased to give it" (v. 21).

Jesus Raises Lazrus From the Grave in Bethany (11:1-44)

The ultimate healing occurs at Bethany near Jerusalem. Jesus says, "I am the resurrection and the life" (v. 25) and then proves it by raising his friend Lazarus from the dead (vv. 38-44). "Lazarus, come out!" Jesus says, and the dead man lives again (v. 43). By combining the resurrection of Lazarus with the "I am" saying, Jesus shows that he is the bestower of eternal life.

"You can no more save a fellow sinner," Charles Haddon Spurgeon once thundered, "than you can create even a small insect, such as a fly." Of course Spurgeon, the great British preacher, knew well the message of Jesus' raising Lazarus. Realizing that God does a work of creation when he saves anyone, Spurgeon knew that God alone grants new life to the spiritually dead. Someone will protest, "If God does it all, then why should I tell others of Christ?" Since Spurgeon personally led thousands to Christ, he is well qualified to teach us that God has seen fit to use the witness of redeemed sinners to bring others to himself. May God use you and me to accomplish that important work!

As Jesus' revelation of himself progresses, the healings increase in difficulty. Jesus heals the nobleman's son who is near death (4:46-54), and then a man who has been lame for thirty-eight years (5:1-15). Finally he raises a man from the grave (11:1-44)! These physical healings portray Jesus as the giver of eternal life.

Jesus Feeds the Five Thousand by Multiplying the Loaves and Fish (6:1-15)

After multiplying the loaves and fish to feed the hungry multitude (6:11), Jesus proclaims: "I am the bread of life. He who comes to me will never go hungry, and he who believes in me will never be thirsty" (v. 35). Just as the bread provides physical sustenance for the crowd, so Jesus gives spiritual life to all who believe in him.

Jesus Raises Himself From the Dead (20:1-29)

We now come to the most important sign—Jesus' resurrection from the dead. Although John never says it explicitly, he gives three hints that Jesus' own resurrection is a sign.

Hint 1: Jesus' Prediction in John 2:19.   After turning the water into wine, Jesus goes to Jerusalem and cleanses the temple. Questioning his authority the Jewish leaders demand, "What miraculous sign can you show us to prove your authority to do all this?" (2:18). By replying, "Destroy this temple, and I will raise it again in three days," Jesus predicts his resurrection from the dead (2:19-22). In response to a demand for a sign, Jesus foretells his resurrection.

Hint 2: Lazarus's Resurrection.   The arrangement of the signs also suggests that Jesus' resurrection is a sign. Only a portion of Jesus' miracles are included in the fourth Gospel (20:30). Although John presents seven signs in chapters 2-11, he records no more until Jesus' resurrection in chapter 20. Therefore, Lazarus's resurrection stands out as the last and greatest of the first seven signs. The absence of any more signs until Jesus raises himself in chapter 20 is conspicuous. We are meant to see Lazarus's resurrection as a pre-view of Jesus' own resurrection.

Hint 3: The "Other" of John 20:30-31.   Furthermore, John 20:30-31 does not make sense unless it is closely preceded by a sign. "Jesus did many other miraculous signs in the presence of his disciples, which are not recorded in this book . . ." (v. 30). Why the word "other"? It makes little sense if the closest sign is the resurrection of Lazarus in chapter 11. However, there is a sign that directly pre-cedes 20:30-31—Jesus' resurrection.

Besides the three hints in the Gospel of John, we can add the testimonies of Matthew 12:38-41 and Luke 11:29-32, where Jesus relates his resurrection to "the sign of the prophet Jonah: For as Jonah was three days and three nights in the belly of a huge fish, so the Son of Man will be three days and three nights in the heart of the earth" (Matt. 12:39-40).

Jesus' resurrection fulfills his predictions in 2:19-22 and 10:17-18, thereby proving himself to be the *revealer of God.* By raising himself from the dead, our Lord also shows that he is the only *Savior* (the subject of our next chapter). Above all, Jesus' resurrection proves that he is the *life-giver.* Prior to his death Jesus said to his disciples, "Before long, the world will not see me anymore, but you will see me. Because I live, you also will live" (14:19). The risen Christ appears to believers; the world in general does not see him. Because of Jesus' resurrection, his disciples gain eternal life. Praise God that Jesus who was crucified is alive and is the source of spiritual life for all who truly believe in his name!

Review Questions
1. Describe the irony in John 9.
2. Show how the increase in the difficulty of Jesus' healings

makes it progressively clearer that he is the life-giver.

3. Explain Jesus' statement in John 6:35.

4. Summarize John's three hints that Jesus' resurrection is a sign.

5. Explain how Jesus' resurrection proves he is revealer, Savior, and life-giver.

Discussion Questions

1. Interpret the difficult John 9:39-41 passage in your own words. Do you know people who falsely claim they can see? How can we help them?

2. Tell how John 5:21 helps us understand the significance of Jesus' healing the lame man by the pool. What Bible study tool could you use for help in answering this question?

3. Jesus' words and deeds are inseparable. Demonstrate this from John 11.

4. If God alone gives spiritual life to sinners, why do we share our faith with them?

5. We often correctly link our receiving eternal life with Jesus' death on the cross. How is Jesus' resurrection also the source of our spiritual life?

5

Jesus' Miraculous "Signs" (2)

Jesus' nine signs are bright stars burning in the dark sky of first-century Palestine. In the previous chapter we began to behold these stars; here we will complete the task. Our Lord's changing water into wine (2:1-11), rescuing the disciples on the Sea of Galilee (6:16-21), and granting the miraculous catch of fish (21:1-14) all present him as Savior.

Jesus, the Savior

Jesus Turns Water Into Wine at the Wedding in Cana (2:1-11)
Jesus, his disciples, and his mother are attending a wedding in Cana of Galilee, when Mary informs her son that the wine has run out (vv. 1-3). Jesus thus tells the servants at the feast to fill six stone jars with water and to take the drink to the master of the banquet. When the servants obey, the master tastes the wine Jesus has made and commends the bridegroom for its excellent quality (vv. 7-10).

Then we read: "This, the first of his miraculous signs, Jesus performed in Cana of Galilee. He thus revealed his glory, and his disciples put their faith in him" (v. 11). How does Jesus show his glory in this sign? A hint is given in John's remark that the water jars were used for Jewish purification rites (v. 6). Jesus is the one who will make the Jewish rites of ceremonial cleansing obsolete. Being the Savior, he will make full and final atonement for sin (see 1:29) so that Jewish purification rites will no longer have any value.

This may sound strange to someone unaccustomed to John's

symbolism. Yet I believe this interpretation is correct for three reasons.

Reason 1: The Spiritual Significance of the Signs.   None of Jesus' nine signs is intended merely to show that he has power over nature. Rather, the signs are spiritual in purpose—they bring about faith in Jesus (20:30-31). While they do show Jesus' power over creation, they go beyond this and show him as revealer, Savior, and giver of life too.

Reason 2: Jesus' Saying in Mark 2:18-22.   John apparently wants his readers to remember a saying from Mark 2:18-22 in conjunction with this sign.

> Now John's disciples and the Pharisees were fasting. Some people came and asked Jesus, "How is it that John's disciples and the disciples of the Pharisees are fasting, but yours are not?" Jesus answered, "How can the guests of the bridegroom fast while he is with them? They cannot, so long as they have him with them. But the time will come when the bridegroom will be taken from them, and on that day they will fast. No one sews a patch of unshrunk cloth on an old garment. If he does, the new piece will pull away from the old, making the tear worse. And no one pours new wine into old wineskins. If he does, the wine will burst the skins, and both the wine and the wineskins will be ruined. No, he pours new wine into new wineskins."

Jesus not only preaches this message, he also acts it out at the wedding in Cana. Fulfilling the bridegroom's responsibility, Jesus provides wine at the wedding. (Recall John 2:10 where the master of the banquet compliments the groom for the good wine.) Here in seed form is the New Testament picture of the church and Christ as bride and groom. Since Jesus is the groom, the Savior of his bride the church, he provides the wine of the wedding feast for her.

John appears to be reminding his readers of Jesus' teaching about the new wine bursting the old wineskins. Taking the jars used for ceremonial washing, Jesus brings forth from them the new wine of the kingdom of God. He thus turns the waters of Jewish purification into the wine of the wedding feast of the groom (Christ) and his bride (the church). He thereby shows the rites of Jewish cleansing to be obsolete.

Reason 3: The Pattern of John 2-4.   This interpretation of the first sign is further confirmed by the pattern in 2:1–4:54. In his earthly ministry Jesus prefigures the missionary progress predicted in Acts 1:8. "But you will receive power when the Holy Spirit comes on you; and you will be my witnesses in Jerusalem, and in all Judea and Samaria, and to the ends of the earth."

Jesus' movements in John 3-4 anticipate the commission given in Acts 1:8. After Jesus talks to Nicodemus in *Jerusalem* (John 3:1-21), the scene shifts to *Judea*, where John the Baptist testifies about Jesus (3:22-36). Thereafter, Jesus ministers in *Samaria*—first to the Samaritan woman and then to the men of Sychar (John 4:1-42). Next in *Galilee* a nobleman's son is healed at Jesus' word (4:43-54). From a Jewish perspective, going from Jerusalem to Galilee represents a movement toward "the ends of the earth." A diagram will help.

Acts 1:8	*John 3-4*
the apostles will take the gospel to	*Jesus ministers in*
● Jerusalem	● Jerusalem (3:1-21)
● Judea	● Judea (3:22-36)
● Samaria	● Samaria (4:1-42)
● the ends of the earth	● Galilee (4:43-54)

What does this have to do with Jesus' turning water into wine? Preceding the expansion of the church outlined in Acts 1:8 were our Lord's death and resurrection. Furthermore, Jesus predicts his resurrection in John 2:12-25 (which directly precedes 3:1-21) when he says, "Destroy this temple, and I will raise it again in three days" (v. 19). Therefore, when 2:1-11 is understood to refer to Jesus' death, the pattern is completed. John designed 2:1–4:54 as follows:

Christ's Saving Work	
and Acts 1:8	*John 2-4*
● Jesus' crucifixion	● Jesus turns water into wine (2:1-11).

- Jesus' resurrection

- Apostolic preaching in
  Jerusalem
  Judea
  Samaria
  the ends of the earth

- Jesus cleanses the temple
  (2:12-25).

- Jesus ministers in
  Jerusalem (3:1-21).
  Judea (3:22-36).
  Samaria (4:1-42).
  Galilee (4:43-54).

Thus when he changes water into wine, Jesus manifests his glory as the Savior who will replace the Jewish ceremonial washings with his atoning death. Thanks be to God that Jesus' death still takes aways sins today!

Searching for spiritual reality, Harry experimented with many religious practices. His wife Judy patiently endured as his pilgrimage led him from one guru to the next. She reached her limit and thought he was losing his sanity, however, when she discovered him sitting cross-legged in their bedroom trying to hear the sound of one hand clapping!

Mercifully, a friend shared the good news of Jesus Christ with Harry and Judy. The turning point came when they understood that only Jesus' atonement—his receiving on the cross the penalty due their sins—could bring them peace with God. Today Harry and Judy are serving the Lord and telling others that Jesus is the Savior of the world.

Jesus Rescues His Disciples on the Sea of Galilee (6:16-21)

Having gone down to the Sea of Galilee at evening, the disciples climb into a boat and start off across the lake for Capernaum. It is dark and Jesus is not with them (6:17). Moreover, the text says, "A strong wind was blowing and the waters grew rough" (v. 18). It is a perilous situation such as that described in Matthew 14:22-33 and Mark 6:45-52.

After rowing approximately three miles, the disciples see Jesus coming near the boat walking on the water. Knowing that they are terrified, Jesus comforts them by saying, "It is I; don't be afraid" (6:20). They take him into the boat, and we are told, "Immediately the boat reached the shore where they were heading" (v. 21). Apparently Jesus miraculously causes the boat to reach their destination at Capernaum.

Without Jesus the disciples were in great danger. After he walked upon the water and they took him aboard, he saved them. Again, this miracle not only shows Jesus' authority over creation. By recording this rescue of the twelve disciples at sea, John presents Jesus as Savior from spiritual danger as well.

In his book *The Persecutor* (Revell, 1973), Sergei Kourdakov tells of his former life as a member of the secret police in Russia. Assigned to forcibly break up the meetings of Christians, he inflicted terrible beatings on them. Sergei describes one of the raids.

> We charged in with all our might, cursing and shoving the Believers to the floor.
>
> I spotted a man in the corner of the room. He had a Bible in his hand and was looking about with terror in his face, trying to find someplace to hide it. Rushing over to him, I grabbed at it roughly, but he held on. I jerked it again and tore it out of his hands. . . . I started ripping the pages out of the Bible, flinging them to the floor. The man, about sixty-five years old, looked up and cried with a pleading tone, "Don't! Please don't! I beg you!"
>
> His mouth was open, begging, and I whirled around, smashing my fist at his face. My fist landed on the edge of his nose and his upper row of teeth. His nose and mouth began to spurt blood. He struggled back to his feet, grabbing the Bible from my hand.
>
> What kind of a fool is he? I asked myself. He values this book more than he values his face! I ripped it away from him again and smashed him again in the face. This time he reeled and fell to the ground unconscious. He wouldn't give us any more trouble. Now my hand was covered with that fool's blood.

Every week Sergei took part in these raids as the KGB tried to keep Christianity from spreading. On one occasion, ordered to burn confiscated Scripture portions, Sergei hid a few pages of Luke's Gospel in his shirt pocket out of curiosity. Later that night alone on his bunk he read them and was deeply affected by Jesus' telling his followers to love their enemies. "Suddenly the words leaped out of those pages and into my heart. . . . It was as though somebody were in the room with me, teaching me those words and what they said. They made a profound impact on me" (p. 176).

Sergei realized that the believers put into practice these teachings of Jesus. He remembered them praying for him even as he was beating them. Gradually the love of the Christians for him, their tormenter, got to Sergei. He found he could no longer take part in the attacks upon believers.

He realized the spiritual danger that surrounded him. Living in an atheistic atmosphere and being a persecutor of Christians, how could he possibly become a believer himself?

Nevertheless, he came to fear the judgment of God more than that of men. To gain freedom he risked his life by diving from a Soviet ship off British Columbia and swimming in icy waters to Canada. By God's grace Sergei trusted Christ as Savior. Later he effectively ministered to youth until he was "mysteriously" shot to death on a skiing trip. In spite of having predicted that the KGB would kill him, Sergei served Christ to the end. Now he enjoys the presence of his Savior in heaven.

Do you find yourself in spiritual danger as Sergei did? Does it seem that you could never become a believer? The answer to your problem is the same as Sergei's. You must look away from your circumstances to Jesus who alone can rescue sinners.

Jesus Gives the Disciples a Miraculous Catch of Fish (21:1-14)

The miraculous catch of fish on the Sea of Galilee (21:1-14) likewise shows Jesus to be the Savior. Three appearances of the risen Lord to his disciples are given in John: (1) to the ten disciples without Thomas (20:19-23; Judas had committed suicide, Matt. 27:5), (2) to the eleven disciples a week later (John 20:24-29), and (3) to the seven disciples by the Sea of Galilee where Jesus granted the wondrous catch of fish (21:1-13; see v. 14 where John labels it the third appearance).

Although the seven disciples have fished all night, they have caught nothing. Early in the morning Jesus stands on the shore and tells them to throw the net on the right side of the boat. In spite of not recognizing him, they obey. As a result, "they were unable to haul the net in because of the large number of fish" (21:3-6).

Because Jesus performed the same miracle before (see Luke 5:1-

11), John tells Peter, "It is the Lord!" (John 21:7). Immediately Peter dives into the water and swims toward Jesus. The disciples, meanwhile, row ashore dragging the net full of 153 large fish. When they land, they meet their Lord and eat breakfast together (vv. 7-13).

Here John invites us to think of Luke 5:1-10, where Jesus gets into Peter's boat and asks him to put out a little from the shore on the Sea of Galilee. After teaching from the boat, Jesus tells Peter, "Put out into deep water, and let down the nets for a catch" (v. 4). Peter first protests, "Master, we've worked hard all night and haven't caught anything." Then he yields, "But because you say so, I will let down the nets" (v. 5). When the disciples obey, we learn that "they caught such a large number of fish that their nets began to break" (v. 6). Then Jesus declares, "From now on you will catch men" (v. 10), which should remind us of Mark 1:17: "Come, follow me, and I will make you fishers of men."

Not only does Jesus proclaim the message of Luke 5:10 and Mark 1:17; in John he acts it out for his disciples after his resurrection. Without Jesus they fish all night and catch nothing; with him they catch many fish. It is the Master's way of teaching that only he can make them effective fishers of men. The point of the miracle is not just that Jesus rules the sea. Being an acted missionary parable, it teaches that Jesus alone is Savior.

The verses that follow in John 21 support this interpretation. When Jesus exhorts Peter to feed his sheep and lambs, "sheep" and "lambs" refer to people. In 21:1-14 Jesus uses the word "fish" to refer to people too. By giving his disciples the miraculous catch of fish, Jesus teaches them about evangelism. In 21:15-17 he teaches Peter and the disciples about their pastoral responsibility. Evangelism (21:1-14) must precede discipleship (21:15-17).

We know that only the blood (the saving death) of Jesus can wash away our sins. We sometimes forget, though, that God must also prepare hearts for people to be saved. When the apostle Paul witnessed to Lydia, the seller of purple, in Philippi, "the Lord opened her heart to respond to Paul's message" (Acts 16:14). John Newton's "Amazing Grace!" one of the world's best-loved hymns, captures this truth in the second stanza.

'Twas grace that taught my heart to fear,
And grace my fears relieved;
How precious did that grace appear
The hour I first believed!

May God strengthen our witness by convincing us that only Jesus makes our evangelism successful. Only he makes us effective fishers of men.

During a recent auto trip to Florida, over a fifty-mile stretch our family was bombarded by humorous signs advertising a place called South of the Border. It seemed a sign popped up every hundred yards on Interstate 95. One, for example, made a pun on "Pedro's" Hispanic pronunciation of English. The sign advertising good food read, "Pedro sez, 'Eat eez wize to come South of the Border.' " Because of the exaggerated claims of the signs, we expected to find a combination of the Taj Mahal, Disneyland, and the Bronx Zoo. Of course, we were disappointed when we finally arrived. No place could live up to those signs!

A different kind of "sign" appears in John—Jesus' nine sign-miracles, which point to himself. Unlike exaggerated advertisements, Jesus does not disappoint us. Even today he is the revealer of God to us who once lived in spiritual darkness. He is still the Savior who saves to the uttermost all who come to God by believing in him. In our day, as two thousand years ago, Jesus grants eternal life to sinners who are spiritually dead. May God increase our appreciation of and devotion to the Lord Jesus Christ.

Review Questions

1. Which signs present Jesus as Savior?

2. How does Mark 2:18-22 help us understand Jesus' turning water into wine in John 2?

3. Show how the pattern of John 2:1–4:54 parallels Jesus' death, resurrection, and the church's mission given in Acts 1:8. How does this pattern help us understand Jesus' turning water into wine?

4. What is the significance of Jesus' walking on the water?

5. The Gospel of John often builds on the first three Gospels.

Show how John 21 builds on Luke 5:1-10.

Discussion Questions

1. Do any of Jesus' signs in John merely show his power over creation? Explain your answer.

2. What do we mean when we say that Jesus made atonement? How does his atonement help us?

3. What encouragement to evangelism is offered by the miraculous catch of fish in John 21?

4. How can our study of Jesus' signs increase our confidence in him?

5. What principles of Bible study can you glean from this chapter?

6

Jesus' "Time" Sayings

"Here we go, honey," Matt said to his wife Sue. "I sure hope this little fella sleeps better than Josh did."

"Believe me, so do I," responded Sue.

The Hopkins were expressing understandable anxiety as they took their newborn son Nathan home from the hospital. Their firstborn, Josh, operating on his own timetable, had upset the family sleeping patterns for two years. The question was, Would baby Nathan follow the same pattern as brother Josh? How thankful the Hopkins were as Nathan quickly adjusted to his family's timetable, sleeping through the night almost from the beginning.

Jesus always lived according to God the Father's timetable. In the Gospel of John this timetable is indicated by means of numerous "time" sayings. Examples include the statements of Jesus such as, "The right time for me has not yet come" (7:6) and "Father, the time has come" (17:1). For ease of study I have grouped similar "time" sayings together into five categories, which form the outline of this chapter:

- The Time of Jesus' Public Manifestation
  Jesus with his mother (2:4)
  Jesus with his brothers (7:6, 8)
- The Time of the Father's Protection of the Son
  "No one laid a hand on him" (7:30)
  "No one seized him" (8:20)
- The Times Present and Future
  With the woman at the well (4:21, 23)
  The dead will live (5:25, 28-29)
- The Time of Jesus' Glorification
  Now the time has come (12:23, 27-28)

53

      A definition (13:1)
      Jesus' priestly prayer (17:1)
- The Time of Persecution for the Disciples
      The disciples' appointed time (16:2, 4, 25, 29, 32)

The Time of Jesus' Public Manifestation

Jesus With His Mother (2:4)

Many Bible students have been perplexed by John 2:4. At the wedding in Cana, after Jesus' mother informs him that the wine has run out, he responds, "My time has not yet come." He seems to be saying that it is not the right time for him to do anything about the wine shortage, but he then proceeds to turn the water into wine. How can Jesus' words (saying that his time has not come) and his actions (turning the water into wine anyway) be reconciled?

The answer to this question is that Jesus is not speaking here about the time to turn water into wine. Rather, he speaks of the time appointed for him to make his full public disclosure to the nation of Israel—a disclosure that will ultimately lead to his death and resurrection.

In John 2:4 Jesus says in effect: "Mother, please do not push me into the limelight. I must carefully follow my heavenly Father's plan. And this is not the time for my great public appearance that will lead to my crucifixion. No, mother, that will happen at my triumphal entry into Jerusalem later in my public ministry."

It was indeed time for Jesus to do his first sign by changing water into wine, but it was not time for him to present himself publicly as Messiah in Jerusalem. This was to occur later according to the plan of God the Father.

Jesus With His Brothers (7:6, 8)

Because the Jewish leaders there want to kill him, Jesus is avoiding Judea (7:1). When the Feast of Tabernacles draws near, his brothers mock him. "You ought to leave here and go to Judea, so that your disciples may see the miracles you do. No one who wants to become a public figure acts in secret. Since you are doing these things, show yourself to the world" (vv. 3-4). Contrary to many readers' first impressions, Jesus' brothers do not say these words in faith. Verse 5 reads, "For even his own brothers did not believe in him."

"The right time for me has not yet come; for you any time is right," Jesus replies (v. 6). This is not Jesus' appointed time. His brothers, however, are not concerned about God's timing, since they are evildoers who belong to the world. Although the world could not hate his brothers, it hates Jesus because he criticizes its sins (v. 7).

Therefore, Jesus tells his brothers to go up to the feast; he will not go up because his time has not yet come. But after his brothers go away, Jesus goes to the feast "not publicly, but in secret" (v. 10). Only when the feast is half over does he begin to teach in public (v. 14).

This "time" saying is similar in meaning to that of 2:4—the time for Jesus' public manifestation in Jerusalem at his triumphal entry (12:12-19) has not yet come. Since he does not want to fall into the hands of his enemies too soon, Jesus goes up to the feast in secret and waits until the middle of the feast to begin teaching publicly.

Both 2:4 and 7:6, 8 must be read with the larger context of Jesus' ministry in mind. It *is* time for him to perform his first sign by turning water into wine. Later, it *is* time for him to go up to the Feast of Tabernacles secretly. However, in both cases it is *not* the Father's appointed time for Jesus to make his great public appearance in Jerusalem leading to his death. Ultimately, it is God's will for him to die, but Jesus has to follow the Father's timetable. And the time has not yet come.

"Hello, my name is Linda. You haven't met me yet. I just wanted to call and tell you that you are the person to lead a Bible study in my home." You can imagine how surprised I was to receive this phone call early in my ministry as an assistant pastor. "I have been praying for years that God would allow me to have a Bible study in my home to reach my unsaved friends. I am convinced that you are the person to lead it," she continued.

Well, it was hard to argue with that. So, after thinking and praying about it for a few days, I told Linda I would be glad to try. After we set a date, she invited her friends and we began. From the first meeting God's hand was upon the Bible study. Since the women eagerly read the appropriate chapter of the Gospel of John each week, we enjoyed lively discussions. Most important, God worked to bring Linda's unsaved friends to faith and to help them grow. This experience taught me to be more sensitive to God's timing.

Are you actively seeking God's timing in your life? When you pray, do you ask him to order your steps so you will follow his timetable?

The Time of the Father's Protection of the Son

"No One Laid a Hand on Him" (7:30)

Twice in John's Gospel we see that although Jesus' enemies want to harm him, they are unable to do so because "his time had not yet come" (7:30 and 8:20). Teaching in the temple courts at the Feast of Tabernacles (7:14-24), Jesus claims that the Father has sent him and that he knows God, but that his hearers do not. "At this they tried to seize him, but no one laid a hand on him, because his time had not yet come" (v. 30).

"No One Seized Him" (8:20)

Preaching to the Jewish leaders, Jesus says, "If you knew me, you would know my Father also" (8:19). The charge that his hearers know neither him nor his Father provokes them. Yet surprisingly they do not arrest him. John 8:20 explains: "He spoke these words while teaching in the temple near the place where the offerings were put. Yet no one seized him, because his time had not yet come."

These two "time" sayings (7:30 and 8:20) highlight the Father's providential protection of Jesus, his unique Son. Although in both cases Jesus' preaching provokes his hearers to wrath, God protects his Son because the appointed time for him to die has not yet come.

It is fascinating to see manifestations of both God's sovereignty and man's responsibility in the fourth Gospel. Since God controls people and circumstances, Jesus is safe in the Father's plan. Nevertheless, the Gospel of John also teaches human responsibility— even Jesus' human responsibility. Notice that John writes in 7:1: "After this, Jesus went around in Galilee, purposely staying away from Judea because the Jews there were waiting to take his life." Although Jesus is safe in God's plan, he does not tempt the Father by acting foolishly. Thus the Father's sovereignty and Jesus' human responsibility exist side by side.

Drawing false conclusions about either God's sovereignty or man's responsibility can hurt our Christian lives. "God is in control," a confused Christian thinks, "so I don't have to pray or tell others of Christ." God is indeed in control; yet he commands us to pray (1 Thess. 5:17) and to witness (Matt. 28:19). According to the Scriptures God's control of all things is not incompatible with his using means to reach his ends. He uses our prayers and our witness to accomplish his will. In fact, because God is sovereign, we are assured of answered prayer and successful evangelism.

Knowing we are responsible for our actions, however, we sometimes seem to forget that God is in charge. Then we try to help him out a bit by worrying. How foolish for us, who are like grasshoppers in his sight, to presume to help the King who sits enthroned above the earth (Isa. 40:22)! Since worrying is contrary to God's will (Matt. 6:34), he commands us to stop worrying and to pray (Phil. 4:6-7).

Many of the early American settlers had firm convictions about the sovereignty of God. When they ventured west in covered wagons, they trusted God to take care of them. However, since they also believed in their human responsibility, they carried firearms to protect their families. Such a combination of trust in divine providence and responsibility to God should mark our lives as well.

The Times Present and Future

With the Woman at the Well (4:21, 23)

After Jesus tells a Samaritan woman about her five husbands and her present immorality (4:16-18), she realizes she is in the presence of a prophet. Diverting attention from her personal life, she says that the Samaritans worship on Mount Gerizim and the Jews in Jerusalem (vv. 19-20).

"Believe me, woman, a time is coming when you will worship the Father neither on this mountain nor in Jerusalem," Jesus replies (v. 21). With these words he predicts a time when true believers will no longer have to make pilgrimages to Jerusalem. This prophecy was fulfilled—when the gospel spread to Jews and Gentiles as recorded in the Book of Acts and the temple was destroyed in A.D. 70. That is why Paul did not tell Gentile Christians to go up to Jerusalem to worship God in one central place; instead, they could do so wherever they lived.

After telling the Samaritan woman that she does not really know what she worships, Jesus declares that salvation comes from the Jews. Then he says an amazing thing. "Yet a time is coming and *has now come* when the true worshipers will worship the Father in spirit and truth . . ." (v. 23). How could Jesus say that the appointed time has already come, when the decentralization of worship is still future? Before the gospel can go to the Gentiles, Jesus has to die, be raised again, ascend to heaven, and pour out the Holy Spirit on the church.

Since Jesus' ministry means the future appointed time has already come, the Samaritan woman does not have to go up to the temple in Jerusalem to worship. She only has to believe in Christ. Jesus' body is the true temple (2:19-22), and what is still future becomes a present reality in him. Thus, there are both present and future aspects to the "time" sayings in chapter 4.

The Dead Will Live (5:25, 28-29)

The same is true with the "time" sayings in chapter 5 as in chapter 4. After Jesus heals a lame man by the pool of Bethesda in Jerusalem (5:1-15), he claims to be the life-giver. "For just as the Father raises the dead and gives them life, even so the Son gives life to whom he is pleased to give it" (v. 21).

A little later he announces, "A time is coming when all who are in their graves will hear his voice [the voice of the Son of man] and come out" (vv. 28-29). Although the righteous will arise to eternal life, the wicked will be raised to condemnation. Pointing to the distant future, Jesus here foretells the resurrection of the dead.

We are perplexed by Jesus' saying in verse 25: "I tell you the truth, a time is coming and *has now come* when the dead will hear the voice of the Son of God and those who hear will live." This verse seems to teach that Jesus would bring about the *physical* resurrection of the dead in his first coming. However, verse 25 must be read in the light of verse 24: "Whoever hears my word and believes him who sent me has eternal life and will not be condemned; he has crossed over from death to life." Therefore, Jesus is speaking of a *spiritual* resurrection in verse 25. Although the time is yet future when he will raise all the dead from their graves, the time has already come when Jesus will give life to the spiritually dead.

Hugh, a good husband and father, was a pleasant fellow to be around. So when Bob came to Hugh's church to begin a discipleship ministry among young adults, he tried to include him. Hugh was too busy at his job for one-on-one Bible study, however, and so Bob worked with others.

A year and a half later Hugh hurt his back and couldn't work for several months. He then told Bob that the time was right for the two of them to meet for a Bible study. As Bob discipled him, Hugh was strengthened in his assurance of salvation.

After Bob moved on to a new ministry, he was surprised and saddened to learn that a blood clot had worked its way into Hugh's heart and killed him. How thankful Bob was for the opportunity to work with Hugh. How mysterious and perfect is God's timing!

The Time of Jesus' Glorification

Now the Time Has Come (12:23, 27-28)

The "time" sayings dramatically shift in chapters 12 and 13. Up until these chapters Jesus' appointed time has not yet come. Now he says, "The hour has come for the Son of Man to be glorified." How will Jesus, the Son of man, be glorified? We usually associate Jesus' glorification with his resurrection, ascension into heaven, sitting at God's right hand, and second coming. But John's view is broader (12:23).

A little parable appears in verse 24. "I tell you the truth, unless a kernel of wheat falls to the ground and dies, it remains only a single seed. But if it dies, it produces many seeds." Since Jesus is here speaking of himself, he is the grain of wheat that dies. Furthermore, his death will win many people for God. After saying that the hour has come for him to be glorified, Jesus tells of his death. He means that he will be glorified in his death on the cross. Admittedly, John does not deny that Christ's glorification includes his resurrection and return to the Father. However, he expands our traditional ideas when he shows us that our Lord's death is a part of his glorification.

John 12:27-28 fits well with this interpretation. "Now my heart is troubled," Jesus says, "and what shall I say? 'Father, save me from this hour?' No, it was for this very reason I came to this hour. Father, glorify your name!" Since the "hour" spoken of here is plainly Jesus' appointed time to die, the "hour" of verse 23 must be the same. And this is the hour for Jesus to be glorified.

Because Jesus is truly human, he admits that his heart is troubled. Nevertheless, he refuses to turn aside from the Father's task for him, for he says, "It was for this very reason I came to this hour" (v. 27). Having come into the world to die for sinners, Jesus will not be swayed from completing his mission. He *will* go to the cross. And there he and the Father will be glorified (vv. 23, 28).

A much-neglected aspect of the Christian life is our motivation. Why are we to live for God? Although the Bible gives us many good reasons (for example, to avoid trouble, to obtain blessing), the greatest motivating force is gratitude to God for our salvation. In fact, here is an inexhaustible source of fuel for our Christian lives. We live for Christ because we are thankful that he did not turn aside from his appointed time to die for us.

A Definition (13:1)

Our Lord's appointed time is defined in 13:1. "Jesus knew that the time had come for him to leave this world and go to the Father." Jesus' appointed time thus includes his death, resurrection, and ascension.

Jesus' Priestly Prayer (17:1)

Praying to God the Father, Jesus says, "Father, the time has come. Glorify your Son, that your Son may glorify you." The "time" here is the same as that of 12:23, 27 and 13:1—it is the time appointed for Jesus to die, rise again, and return to the Father.

John 17:4-5 helps us understand verse 1. The Father will answer Jesus' prayer for glorification (v. 1) by taking him into his presence in heaven (v. 5). And Jesus will glorify the Father (v. 1) by completing God's work (v. 4)—by going to the cross.

The Time of Persecution for the Disciples

The Disciples' Appointed Time (16:2, 4, 25, 29, 32)

In chapter 16 it is not Jesus' appointed time that is in view, but that of his apostles. Jesus warns his disciples of difficult times ahead. "They will put you out of the synagogue; in fact, a time is coming when anyone who kills you will think he is offering a service to God" (v. 2).

Preparing them for the time when he will leave and return to the Father, Jesus tells of coming persecutions. "I have told you this, so that when the time comes you will remember that I warned you" (16:4). Just as Jesus' appointed time involves his death on the cross, so his disciples also have an appointed time of suffering.

Previously Jesus taught his disciples through the use of symbolic statements such as "Destroy this temple, and I will raise it again in three days" (2:19). Now, however, he says, "Though I have been speaking figuratively, a time is coming when I will no longer use this kind of language but will tell you plainly about my Father" (16:25). Since Jesus has begun to teach them plainly already, his disciples are pleased. "Now you are speaking clearly and without figures of speech" (16:29). Their Lord will continue to do so after his resurrection.

Finally, the disciples confess that Jesus comes from God (16:30). "You believe at last!" Jesus says. "But a time is coming, and has come, when you will be scattered, each to his own home. You will leave me all alone. Yet I am not alone, for my Father is with me" (vv. 31-33). When Jesus is arrested, the disciples will leave him (18:8-9). Their time of suffering will begin and continue on after Jesus returns to the Father. In spite of the trouble and persecution that the world will give the disciples, Jesus promises them his lasting joy and peace (16:22, 33).

Like the disciples, we too sometimes must pass through deep waters. What a comfort to know that God is in charge and our lives are in his hands.

The hymn "Give to the Winds Thy Fears" (written in German by Paul Gerhardt and translated by John Wesley) encourages us in difficult times.

> Give to the winds thy fears,
> Hope and be undismayed;
> God hears thy sighs, and counts thy tears,
> God shall lift up thy head,
> Through waves and clouds and storms
> He gently clears the way;
> Wait thou His time, so shall the night
> Soon end in joyous day.

> Still heavy is thy heart?
> Still sink thy spirits down?
> Cast off the weight, let fear depart,
> And every care be gone.
> He everywhere hath sway,
> And all things serve His mind;
> His every act pure blessing is,
> His path unsullied light.

> Far, far above thy thought
> His counsel shall appear,
> When fully He the work hath wrought

That caused thy needless fear.
Leave to His sovereign will
To choose and to command:
With wonder filled, thou then shalt own
How wise, how strong His hand.

All the "time" sayings demonstrate that God has a plan of salvation stretching from Jesus' earthly ministry (4:23; 5:25; 16:25, 29) to the future resurrection of the dead (5:28). This plan involves God's providential protection of His Son (7:30; 8:20), but it does not negate Jesus' human responsibility (7:1). Included in God's plan are Jesus' triumphal entry (2:4; 7:6, 8), the persecution of his followers (16:2, 4, 32), and the decentralization of worship in the church (4:21).

God's plan centers on Jesus' appointed time to go to the cross, rise from the dead, and return to the Father (12:23, 27; 13:1; 17:1). In these events Jesus and the Father will be glorified (12:23; 17:1).

Since God is in control, Jesus must obey the Father and wait for the appointed time (2:4; 7:6, 8). When the time comes, however, nothing can hold Jesus back (12:27-28). Having come to glorify God by finishing His work, Jesus will finish it (17:1, 4).

"Sometimes I feel like giving up, like there is nothing more worth living for," said Edith Hannon, a brave Christian woman. Tim and Edith undoubtedly were an unusual couple. He suffered from throat cancer and couldn't speak. She rode around in a wheelchair. Nevertheless, all who knew them were moved by the way they cared for each other. He was her legs; she was his voice. And they both were full of life. Edith would say, "Pity the poor man who cannot talk . . . married to a woman who talks a mile a minute!" Then Tim would respond with a face that would make anyone laugh.

Things changed. Tim got worse and Edith lost her smile. Withdrawing, she prepared for the inevitable. After his death, she was a different person, for all the joy of life had been squeezed out of her. Although it was hard for her to pray or read her Bible, her friends would not let her give up. They prayed for her and with her. They visited and read the Scriptures with her. Slowly she rebuilt her life, and today she has her old sparkle.

"What kept you going through the dark days and sleepless

nights?" a friend asked her. Edith replied, "I never lost sight of the fact that God has a plan for all things. I thank him for giving me Tim for nine wonderful years. I am now praying that God will show me what he wants me to do with the rest of my life. It is still hard. Some days I would rather go be with Tim. But Jesus is my Lord—and he has me here for a reason."

Review Questions

1. What did Jesus mean in John 2:4 when he said that his time had not yet come?

2. After Jesus told his brothers, "The right time for me has not yet come" (John 7:6), why did he still go up to the Feast of Tabernacles?

3. What did Jesus mean when he told the Samaritan woman that the time had already come when people would worship the Father in spirit and truth (John 4:23)?

4. Explain the present and future dimensions to Jesus' "time" sayings in John 5:25, 28-29.

5. Which saying gives a definition of the most important aspects of Jesus' appointed time? Explain.

Discussion Questions

1. Show how John 7:1, 30, and 8:20 demonstrate God's sovereignty and man's responsibility. How can we neatly fit together God's sovereignty and human responsibility?

2. Tell how being aware of the dramatic shift in the "time" sayings in chapters 12 and 13 can help you interpret John's Gospel.

3. How can Jesus' "time" sayings in chapter 16 give us a realistic view of the Christian life?

4. The overall effect of the "time" sayings is to remind us of God's great plan. How should our awareness of God's plan affect our daily lives?

5. In what ways could you be more sensitive to God's timetable for your life?

7

Conflicting Responses to Jesus

Some cried, "We love him!" Others screamed, "We hate him!" Feelings ran high when C. Everett Koop was appointed Surgeon General of the United States. While pro-lifers hailed the appointment as an answer to prayer, abortionists protested loudly.

Like Dr. Koop many public figures find themselves at the center of controversy. But no one drew such conflicting responses as did the Lord Jesus. In John's Gospel some who hear his words and see his signs put their faith in him for salvation. Others utterly despise and reject him.

The Two Responses in the Prologue

The two opposite responses to Jesus are introduced in the first twelve verses of the fourth Gospel. After telling of the incarnation in verse 9, John writes, "He was in the world, and though the world was made through him, the world did not recognize him. He came to that which was his own, but his own did not receive him" (1:10-11). Although God sent his Son to save the world, most people rejected him!

We gladly read of another response to Jesus' ministry in 1:12. "Yet to all who received him, to those who believed in his name, he gave the right to become children of God." Here is a positive response to Christ—believing in him for salvation. Ultimately this response does not depend upon human will, but is the work of God in man (v. 13).

The entire Gospel of John is summed up for us in 1:10-13. John 1:10-11, which speaks of *unbelief*, corresponds to chapters 2-12. Depicting an unbelieving response to Jesus, this section is summarized in 12:37. "Even after Jesus had done all these miraculous signs in their presence, they still would not believe in him." John 1:12-13, which tells of *belief,* lines up with John 13-20. These chapters are summarized in 20:30-31, which speaks of believing in Jesus for eternal life.

John thus organizes his book on the basis of the two opposing responses to Jesus. In chapters 2-12 the Jewish leaders do not believe in Jesus, even though he delivers God's messages and performs seven miracles. In John 13-20 the disciples believe in Jesus when he teaches them privately and then performs the greatest sign by raising himself from the dead.

The two responses to Jesus in the Gospel of John reflect a pattern deeply ingrained in the Bible. At the time of the flood, "Noah, when warned about things not yet seen, in holy fear built an ark to save his family. By his faith he condemned the world . . ." (Heb. 11:7). Whereas Noah and his family believed in the Lord and were de- livered, the unbelieving world received the judgment of God.

At the time of the Exodus, God enabled the Israelites to pass "through the Red Sea as on dry land; but when the Egyptians tried to do so, they were drowned" (Heb. 11:29). God delivered the Jews who in faith obeyed him and left Egypt. However, he destroyed hardhearted Pharaoh and his soldiers in the sea.

Peter speaks of these contrasting responses when he refers to Christ as a living stone: "Now to you who believe, this stone is precious. But to those who do not believe, 'The stone the builders rejected has become the capstone,' and 'A stone that causes men to stumble and a rock that makes them fall' " (1 Pet. 2:7-8).

This biblical pattern of belief and unbelief holds true today. All who trust Jesus as Savior know that he is precious. But all who turn away from Christ and the salvation he freely offers stumble over him and one day will experience his wrath. If you do not know Jesus, I encourage you to bow before him and believe that he died for your sins and rose to save you.

A Pattern of Alternating Faith and Unbelief
Although unbelief dominates the first half of the Gospel of John

and belief the second half, both are present throughout. Let us study a pattern of alternating belief and unbelief in John 2. After Jesus changes water into wine, we read: "This, the first of his miraculous signs, Jesus performed in Cana of Galilee. He thus revealed his glory, and his disciples put their faith in him" (2:11).

When Jesus cleanses the temple (in the account that immediately follows), the Jewish leaders do not respond with faith in him. Instead, they demand a sign from him to prove his authority to cleanse the temple. Jesus then predicts his resurrection by saying, "Destroy this temple, and I will raise it again in three days" (v. 19). At this the Jews rail at him in amazement and unbelief. In contrast, "after he was raised from the dead, his disciples recalled what he had said. Then they believed the Scripture and the words Jesus had spoken" (v. 22).

The pattern of alternating belief and unbelief appears to be broken in verse 23: "Now while he was in Jerusalem at the Passover Feast, many people saw the miraculous signs he was doing and believed in his name." On closer inspection, however, we learn that the "faith" described in verse 23 is not true saving faith. In fact, it is an example of John's doctrine of false faith, as is proved by verse 24: "But Jesus would not entrust himself to them, for he knew all men." Certainly, Jesus would entrust himself to those who truly believed in him. Thus the so-called believers of verse 23 apparently only believe in Jesus as a miracle worker; they do not discern the spiritual purpose of the signs and trust him as Savior.

We can sketch the pattern as follows:

Passage   *Response to Jesus*
2:1-11   (+) The disciples believe in Jesus.
2:12-21   (–) The Jewish leaders do not believe in Jesus.
2:22   (+) The disciples (will) believe in Jesus.
2:23-24   (–) Many people do not believe in Jesus; they believe falsely.

Nicodemus and the Samaritan Woman

The character studies in chapters 3 and 4 are introduced by John 2:25. "He [Jesus] did not need man's testimony about man, for he knew what was in a man." Since chapter 3 begins with "Now there was a man of the Pharisees named Nicodemus . . . ," John presents Nicodemus as an example of "a man." Nicodemus has all the advantages: he is a Jewish man, a Pharisee, a member of the Sanhedrin (the Jewish ruling body), and a prominent teacher in Israel (vv. 1, 10). Although we would expect him to have the spiritual insight to believe in Jesus, Nicodemus is presented as a seeker who at this point does not believe. In fact, Jesus says that Nicodemus is among those who do not understand spiritual things, do not accept the testimony of the Father and Son, and do not believe (vv. 10, 12).

We are confronted by another specimen of humanity in chapter 4. This one has three strikes against her: she is a woman (rabbis did not talk with women in public, 4:27), a Samaritan ("Jews do not associate with Samaritans," v. 9), and immoral (vv. 16-19). Surely, she will never find favor with God!

However, the Samaritan woman gradually learns Jesus' identity: He is "a Jew" (v. 9), "a prophet" (v. 19), and the Messiah (vv. 25-26). After she says that the Messiah is coming, Jesus replies that he is the Messiah (v. 26). At this she leaves her water jar and goes back to Sychar to tell the people about Jesus. The reason? She has found someone more important than the water she had come to draw from the well—Jesus the Messiah.

In fact, the Samaritan woman appears as an evangelist who testifies of Jesus to the men of Sychar. Because of her witness, they come to hear Jesus and believe in him (vv. 29-30, 39).

The two opposite responses to Jesus in chapters 3 and 4 teach us that God's ways are not ours. He delights to humble the proud (Nicodemus) and to exalt the humble (the Samaritan woman).

Ricky had a terrible reputation in his home town of Olean, New York. He drank heavily, used drugs, and was usually involved in one scrape or another. Stan by contrast seemed to be a model teen-ager. He was clean-cut, had good morals, and was a prominent member of the youth group in a large church in town. Repulsed by Ricky's lifestyle, Stan became angry when some of the kids from his church took an interest in him. "Why do you have time for that guy?" Stan demanded. "He's no good and never will be!" Because the young people respected Stan's opinion, most gave up on Ricky.

A young woman named Eleanor, however, kept praying for the troubled teen-ager. One day her opportunity came to show Christ's love to him. Having been badly hurt in a motorcycle accident, Ricky lay in the hospital, depressed. Eleanor visited him every day for a month. At first he didn't want to see her, but gradually he came to appreciate her concern for him. Being careful not to appeal to Ricky's romantic interests, Eleanor was there as a Christian who cared for him. Ricky had never before met a person like Eleanor. Before long, she got him reading the Word of God, and a few weeks later he entered into a personal relationship with God through Christ.

The people of Olean were stunned by the turnaround in Ricky's life. In fact, many did not even recognize him at first after his conversion. Ricky explained: "Before I came to know the Lord, I was rebellious—and I wanted everybody to know I was rebellious. So I always dressed and acted that way."

Although Ricky was able to influence many others for Christ, one person was not at all happy about Ricky's new life—Stan. He became so upset with all the attention Ricky was getting that he left the church and eventually lost interest in spiritual things. God humbles the proud and exalts the humble.

The Samaritans and the Galileans

The Samaritans and the Galileans in John 4 also demonstrate the two responses to Christ. Although Jesus displays supernatural knowledge when he tells the Samaritan woman "everything [she] ever did" (4:39), he performs no signs in Sychar. Nevertheless, many Samaritans believe in him because of his words. When they hear Jesus' message, they believe in him as "Savior of the world" (vv. 41-42).

At first glance it looks as if the Galileans also believe in Jesus. "When he arrived in Galilee, the Galileans welcomed him. They had seen all that he had done in Jerusalem at the Passover Feast, for they also had been there" (v. 45). However, theirs is not true faith; it is false faith similar to that in 2:23. We should have been tipped off to that by 4:44. "Now Jesus himself had pointed out that a prophet has no honor in his own country." Furthermore, Jesus' words in verse

48 confirm our interpretation. "Unless you people see miraculous signs and wonders you will never believe." How different are the Samaritans who believe in Jesus "because of his words" (v. 41).

Jesus does not do another public sign for the Galileans. Instead, he performs a private miracle for a royal official from Capernaum whose son was near death. In contrast to the sign-seeking Galileans, that official takes "Jesus at his word" (v. 50). Later, when he learns that his boy was healed at the very time Jesus said "Your son will live," the man and his family believe (v. 53).

What about us? Are we sign seekers? Or have we learned the lesson Jesus taught in Matthew 12:39—"A wicked and adulterous generation asks for a miraculous sign"? Please don't misunderstand. I believe that God is able to perform miracles today. In fact, most Christians should believe him for greater things than they do. But there is a great deal of misguided sign seeking today. To cite just one example, much of the religious programming on television trains us to expect a miracle a minute. Such teaching is clearly unbiblical. Faith that glorifies God takes him at his Word. It doesn't seek for signs to prop itself up; it rests in God's promises in the Bible.

When it comes to faith, are you a Samaritan or a Galilean?

Other Examples of the Two Responses

Each of the first twelve chapters of John's Gospel depicts the two responses to Jesus' ministry. After Jesus' message at the Feast of Tabernacles in John 7, for example, some proclaim him the prophet (of Deut. 18:15, 18), and some say he is the Christ (7:40-41). Nevertheless, others are skeptical because they think Jesus does not meet the messianic qualification of being born in Bethlehem (7:42). "Thus the people were divided because of Jesus" (v. 43).

Conflicting responses are also evident at the end of chapter 9 where the blind man whom Jesus has healed worships him (v. 38). In contrast, the Jewish leaders excommunicate the blind man and refuse to see their need for Jesus, the light of the world.

Perhaps the most dramatic example of opposite responses to Jesus occurs in chapter 11. After Jesus raises Lazarus from the dead, many of the Jews put their faith in Christ (11:45). Others, however, go to the Pharisees and report what Jesus has done (v. 46). Then the Jewish leaders meet, and "from that day on they plotted to take his life" (v. 53). It is hard to conceive of two more vastly different responses—believing in Jesus and planning his murder.

Christians sometimes forget Jesus' words:

> Do not suppose that I have come to bring peace to the earth. I did not come to bring peace, but a sword. For I have come to turn "a man against his father, a daughter against her mother, a daughter-in-law against her mother-in-law—a man's enemies will be the members of his own household" (Matt. 10:34-36).

Although many of us may forget these words, Jerry came to know them very well. Jerry felt disoriented after he moved from the country to attend a Christian college in the city. In fact, he did not sleep well the whole first month at college because of the noises at night. The young man was just not used to blaring radios, busy traffic, and people congregating on street corners to talk late into the night.

Adjustment to city life was not Jerry's biggest personal problem, however. Within a few months he learned to like his surroundings, but another difficulty refused to go away. Jerry suffered from a broken heart.

Once part of a close-knit family, he had been crushed when his loved ones not only refused to believe in Jesus, but also disowned him for trusting in Christ as his Lord and Savior. Jerry's heart ached whenever his father's parting words echoed in his mind: "As long as you believe in this religious nonsense, you are no son of mine."

It has been fifteen years since Jerry completed college. He attended seminary and married, and now is pastor of a rural church not far from his home town. I wish I could tell you that his family has been gloriously saved or even that they are now warm toward Jerry, but I can't. Jerry knows personally that Jesus often arouses conflicting responses.

The Disciples Also Will Receive Two Opposing Responses

Jesus applies the idea of the two responses to his disciples in John

15:20. "Remember the words I spoke to you: 'No servant is greater than his master.' If they persecuted me, they will persecute you also. If they obeyed my teaching, they will obey yours also." Here Jesus wisely warns his followers that people will spurn their message just as they did his. Our Lord also promises positive results; just as some obeyed his word, so some will believe the disciples' testimony to him.

Having known the Lord for a little more than a week, Tom already was so discouraged that he felt like giving up his new faith. He had been telling his fellow workers at the tire factory about Jesus, but the rough group of men came down hard on him for "having gotten religion," as they put it. The Christian man who had led Tom to Christ had not prepared him for such a negative response to his witnessing. In fact, Tom had been misled into thinking that the Christian life was all "peaches and cream"—the very words that his spiritual father had used. Well, Tom soon found out otherwise!

Later, a brother in the Lord showed Tom Jesus' teaching in John 15:20 warning us that sometimes our evangelism will not be successful. Encouraged not to give up, Tom continued to pray for his fellow workers. As he resisted the temptation to shun the "heathen," he learned to show concern for them. Gradually others came to Christ through Tom's witness in life and word.

"I will never stop praying for my brother Austin's salvation as long as I live," my friend Newton resolved. And he was true to his word. Newton was the first to come to Christ in a family of four boys. His brother Carl put his faith in Jesus shortly after Newton did, but his brother Austin was another story. Although Newton and Carl spoke to him about the Lord, Austin avoided the claims of Christ upon his life.

Other believers gave up on Austin over the years, but Newton trusted God and kept praying. In 1960, a year before he passed away, Austin Conant trusted Jesus as his Lord and Savior. His brother Newton had prayed for him for over thirty-eight years! May God use Jesus' promise in John 15:20 to help us never give up praying for loved ones as long as they are alive: "If they obeyed my teaching, they will obey yours also."

Incidentally, you may be wondering about the fourth son in the family. Perry has still not come to Christ, but Newton remains faithful in prayer.

The Word of God is realistic—it describes life as it is, including the two opposite responses to Jesus and his followers. God promises that one day "at the name of Jesus every knee should bow . . . and every tongue confess that Jesus Christ is Lord, to the glory of God the Father" (Phil. 2:10-11). But in the meantime many people refuse to bow before Jesus and glorify God.

In the opening stanza of his hymn "At Calvary" William R. Newell reflects back on his own unbelieving response to Christ.

> Years I spent in vanity and pride,
> Caring not my Lord was crucified,
> Knowing not it was for me He died On Calvary.

Thanks to God's grace we need not remain "in vanity and pride" but can join with Newell and sing:

> By God's Word at last my sin I learned;
> Then I trembled at the law I'd spurned,
> Till my guilty soul imploring turned To Calvary.

> Now I've given to Jesus everything;
> Now I gladly own him as my King
> Now my raptured soul can only sing Of Calvary.

> Oh, the love that drew salvation's plan!
> Oh, the grace that brought it down to man!
> Oh, the mighty gulf that God did span At Calvary!

[Refrain]

> Mercy there was great, and grace was free;
> Pardon there was multiplied to me;
> There my burdened soul found liberty, At Calvary.

Review Questions

1. Show how John 1:10-13 outlines the Gospel of John.
2. Summarize the pattern of alternating belief and unbelief in John 2.

3. Explain John 2:23-24 and 4:45.

4. What are other examples of the two responses to Jesus in John's Gospel?

5. Cite other biblical examples of the two responses outside of the Gospel of John.

Discussion Questions

1. Why do you think John organized his Gospel on the basis of the two opposing responses to Jesus? What was he communicating by doing so?

2. Tell how John's presentation of Nicodemus and the Samaritan woman shows that God's ways are not ours. Can you think of examples of this today?

3. Discuss how people today are thought of as being Samaritans or Galileans when it comes to faith. Which are you?

4. What is John's purpose in teaching a doctrine of false faith? How can understanding this doctrine help us today?

5. How does realizing that we, too, will receive contrasting responses help us be both realistic and optimistic while sharing the gospel?

8

Portraits of Jesus' Person (1)

In November of 1986, six paintings were sold at an auction house in London for $24.14 million. The works of art and their prices were *Yo: Picasso,* a self-portrait ($5.83 million), Mondrian's *Composition in a Square With Red Corner* ($5.06 million), Jasper John's *Out the Window* ($3.6 million), Leonardo da Vinci's *Child With a Lamb* ($3.6 million), Renoir's *La Coiffure* ($3.52 million), and Joan Miro's *Woman in the Night* ($2.53 million).

It's doubtful any of us could afford to spend that kind of money. And yet John invites us to enjoy six *priceless* pictures of Jesus—free of charge! John portrays Jesus as the:

- Christ
- Savior
- revealer of God
- Son of God
- life-giver
- Son of man

We will view the first three in this chapter and the remaining three in the next.

The Christ
The first portrait presents Jesus as the Christ who fulfills the Old Testament—and even surpasses it (20:30-31).

Grace and Truth
Already in the prologue we learn that Jesus is the Christ. "For the

75

law was given through Moses; grace and truth came through Jesus Christ" (1:17). Some readers misunderstand this verse, taking it to mean that there are no grace and truth in the Old Testament. In fact, these are Old Testament concepts (see Exod. 34:6; Pss. 25:10; 117:2) that speak of God's loving-kindness ("grace") and faithfulness ("truth").

Actually, John makes an overstated comparison in 1:17. Compared with the loving-kindness and faithfulness of God revealed in Jesus, the Old Testament appears to be only a revelation of law. Since Jesus is the Christ, he far surpasses the Old Testament revelations of God's grace and truth.

Andrew and Philip

Later in John 1, Andrew and Philip confess that Jesus is the Christ. "We have found the Messiah," Andrew says to Peter before he brings him to Jesus (1:41). The next day Philip testifies to Nathanael, "We have found the one Moses wrote about in the Law, and about whom the prophets also wrote—Jesus of Nazareth, the son of Joseph" (1:45).

The True Temple

Predicting his resurrection from the dead, Jesus says, "Destroy this temple, and I will raise it again in three days" (2:19-22). He thereby presents himself as that to which the temple pointed—the ultimate dwelling of God with men. Since Jesus is the true temple, worshipers no longer have to go up to Jerusalem (4:21-24). Instead, through Jesus they can worship God spiritually ("in spirit") and in accordance with God's will ("in truth") regardless of location. The future decentralization of worship (described in Acts) has already become a present reality in Jesus' earthly ministry.

The Great Men of the Old Testament

Jesus also supersedes the great personalities of the Old Testament. As we have already seen, he is greater than Moses (1:17).

Furthermore, every Christian reader knows how to answer the Samaritan woman's question to Jesus, "Are you greater than our father Jacob . . . ?" (4:12). In addition, since Isaiah "saw Jesus' glory and spoke about him" (12:41), he is greater than Isaiah. In fact, he is even greater than Abraham, for Jesus could say, "Before Abraham was born, I am!" (8:58), claiming to be the great I AM of Exodus 3:14.

The Theme of the Old Testament

Among the many witnesses to Jesus—John the Baptist, Jesus' miracles, God the Father—are the Old Testament Scriptures (5:31-47). In fact, Jesus is the theme of the Old Testament. His words are filled with irony, therefore, when he tells the Jews that they do not believe Moses' writings because they do not believe in him (vv. 45-47). Admittedly, the Jewish authorities love the law of Moses; but, since they do not accept Jesus as the Christ, they do not understand the Old Testament correctly. The law becomes an instrument of death for them, because they refuse to believe in the Christ to whom it points. This is what Jesus means when he says that Moses, on whom the Jewish leaders have set their hope, will actually be their accuser.

Other Examples

In fact, Jesus is presented as the Christ in almost every chapter of John's Gospel. The manna given from heaven in ancient Israel's wilderness wanderings is a picture of Jesus, the true manna (6:32-33, 48-51) who gives spiritual life to all who "eat" (believe in) him. Although the fathers ate the manna in the desert and died, the one who eats this living bread will not die, but live forever (6:49-51).

Furthermore, Jesus is a descendant of David and was born in Bethlehem (7:42). When the crowd hears his sermon at the Feast of Tabernacles, some reject him. The reason for their rejection? They thought he failed to satisfy the requirements for messiahship—lineage from David and birth in Bethlehem. We say to ourselves, "But he *is* a descendant of David and he *was* born in Bethlehem!" Thus with irony John shows that Jesus meets the requirements.

Replacing the nation of Israel, who failed in its duty to be a light to the Gentiles, Jesus is the true light of the world (9:5). Unlike the false shepherds of Israel, he is the true shepherd (10:11). While the Old Testament *prophesied* the resurrection of the dead (Dan. 12:2), Jesus *is* the resurrection and the life (11:24-27). And being the true vine, he takes over the task that Israel, the vineyard of the Lord, failed to accomplish (15:1).

Raised in an Orthodox Jewish home, Sharon married a Gentile, who agreed to adopt a Jewish lifestyle. Her husband felt that her faith gave stability to their family, and he even encouraged their daughter to attend Hebrew Academy. Over the years as he became active in Jewish social concerns and learned to love the Jewish people, he decided to convert to Judaism. For an adult male to do so he must (1) be circumcised, or if already circumcised, let a rabbi draw a little blood from his finger, (2) undergo a ritual cleansing bath, and (3) renounce all other faiths.

"Naturally you'll have to renounce Jesus," Sharon said matter-of-factly as they discussed his desire to convert.

"I don't think I can do that," he replied.

Shocked by her husband's stand, she vowed to disprove that Jesus was the Messiah. Enlisting the help of numerous rabbis, she painstakingly studied the Bible and Talmud. Yet, after a year she had not succeeded. In fact, she now had many unanswered questions about Jesus. So the rabbis steered her to another rabbi, who specialized in helping Jews refute Christianity.

But an amazing thing happened as she studied with him. The more Sharon studied, the more she became convinced Jesus is the Messiah! Finally, both she and her husband put their faith in Jesus. Contrary to her original intention, Sharon had come to realize that Jesus is the Christ who fulfilled, and went beyond, the Old Testament (Sharon Allen, *The Chosen People* [July 1987], pp. 7-9).

If you are Jewish, I invite you to examine the claims of Jesus for yourself. The best way to do that is to study three New Testament documents: the Gospel of Matthew, the Epistle to the Hebrews, and the very book we are studying now, the Gospel of John.

The Savior

John's second portrait of Jesus shows him as the Savior of the world.

> For God so loved the world that he gave his one and only Son, that whoever believes in him shall not perish but have eternal life. For God did not send his Son into the world to condemn the world, but to save the world through him. Whoever believes in him is not condemned, but whoever does not believe stands condemned already because he has not believed in the name of God's one and only Son (John 3:16-18).

Having compassion on a world desperately in need of salvation, the Father sent the Son of God to rescue people from their sins. While those who believe in him as Savior have eternal life, those who reject him are already condemned, because they are sinners and have not availed themselves of God's only remedy.

The "I Am" Sayings

Jesus is also Savior as seen in two of the "I am" sayings. In 10:7, 9 Jesus is the gate who alone gives access to the true people of God (see pp. 29-30). In 14:6 he is the only way to the Father's house in heaven (see p. 29). Since Jesus alone is able to rescue sinners, the gospel message is urgent. We must warn others that unless they trust him as their Savior, they will die in their sins (8:21, 24).

The Signs

Likewise, three of the signs picture Jesus as Savior. When he turns the water into wine, he shows that his death would make atonement for sins, thereby replacing the Jewish purification rites (2:1-11; see pp. 44-47).

By rescuing his disciples from danger on the Sea of Galilee, he demonstrates that he is Savior from spiritual danger (6:16-21: see pp. 47-48).

Without Jesus the disciples fish all night and catch nothing. With him, however, they catch many fish, because only the Savior can make them effective fishers of men (21:1-14; see pp. 49-50).

An Invitation
    Dear reader, if you have not yet had your sins forgiven, I invite you now to trust Jesus as Savior. You must put away any self-effort for salvation, since you cannot rescue yourself. Instead, you must look away from yourself and believe in Jesus to be saved (3:16). Specifically, you must believe that Jesus died on the cross to take away your sins (1:29). If you do, John's purpose in writing the Gospel will be fulfilled in your life. And you will then be able to sing Elisha A. Hoffman's hymn "What a Wonderful Saviour!":

> Christ has for sin atonement made,
>   What a wonderful Saviour!
> We are redeemed! The price is paid!
>   What a wonderful Saviour!
>
> I praise Him for the cleansing blood,
>   What a wonderful Saviour!
> That reconciled my soul to God;
>   What a wonderful Saviour!
>
> He cleansed my heart from all its sin,
>   What a wonderful Saviour!
> And now He reigns and rules therein;
>   What a wonderful Saviour!

[Refrain]

> What a wonderful Saviour is Jesus, my Jesus!
> What a wonderful Saviour is Jesus, my Lord!

The Revealer of God

The Word and the True Light
    The third portrait is painted first in 1:1-5, 14 where Jesus is called

the Word. As we communicate our thoughts to others through words, so God expressed his mind through his Word, Jesus Christ. Even before the incarnation, the Word revealed God by virtue of the things the Word had made (1:3-4). Later as the incarnate Word, Jesus revealed the glory, grace, and truth of God (v. 14).

When John says that Jesus is the true light, he means that he is the revealer of God. Even as light illumines that on which it shines, so Jesus, the true light, comes into the world and illumines every person he encounters during his earthly ministry (1:9).

The prologue concludes with another statement that shows Jesus as the heavenly revealer: "No one has ever seen God, but God the One and Only, who is at the Father's side, has made him known" (1:18). God, who is spirit, is of course invisible; Jesus, however, through his character, speech, and actions makes the invisible God visible.

The "I Am" Sayings

Two of the "I am" sayings also teach that Jesus reveals the Father to the world. When Jesus says "I am the light of the world" (9:5) and then gives sight to the blind man, he shows that he is the illuminator (see pp. 27-28).

When Jesus says "I am the truth" in 14:6, he means that he has come from God to bring God's truth to people. Similarly he says to Pilate, "In fact, for this reason I was born, and for this I came into the world, to testify to the truth" (18:37; see p. 27).

Other Sayings of Jesus

The fourth Gospel is filled with Jesus' sayings showing he is the revealer of God. "My teaching is not my own," he says. "It comes from him who sent me" (7:16). Moreover, he tells his foes, "I am telling you what I have seen in the Father's presence" (8:38). Later Jesus says, "I did not speak on my own accord, but the Father who sent me commanded me what to say and how to say it. I know that his command leads to eternal life. So whatever I say is just what the Father has told me to say" (12:49-50).

Jesus' Divine and Human Natures

No one who saw the centennial lighting of the Statue of Liberty will soon forget it. All was dark except for a few specks of light from remote stars. Then, with the flick of a switch the giant lights came on, and the darkness was overcome by the brilliance of Lady Liberty dominating the harbor. So it is with the ministry of Jesus, the revealer of God. The previous revelation of God appears as darkness in comparison with his brilliant light. Jesus sheds light on the character and will of God the Father as never before.

This is one of the perspectives from which John teaches Christ's deity and humanity. As God, the heavenly revealer comes from the Father to the world to reveal *God* to men; who can better reveal God than God himself? As a genuine human being, Jesus reveals God to *men;* who can better do this than a human being? Jesus is thus the divine-human revealer of the Father.

May Jesus' revelation of the Father renew our reading of the Gospels! As we read them let us pray, "Father, make yourself known to us through the words and deeds of Jesus, the revealer."

Review Questions

1. Does John 1:17 criticize the Old Testament? Explain.
2. How are we to understand Jesus' cryptic words in John 2:19?
3. Show the irony in John 5:46-47.
4. Which signs and "I am" sayings show Jesus is Savior?
5. What does John 1 mean when it calls Jesus "the Word"?

Discussion Questions

1. Tell how Jesus supersedes the great personalities of the Old Testament. What place should he have in your personal life? In your family life? In your church life? How can you better give him the place he deserves?

2. Using the Bible are you able to show a Jewish friend that Jesus is the Messiah? Make a list of the places in John where Jesus is presented as the Christ.

3. We all need to be more excited about the fact that Jesus is our

Savior. Take a few minutes to thank Jesus for being such a wonderful Savior. You may want to use the song in this chapter to help you do so.

4. Explain how Jesus' deity and humanity qualify him to be the ultimate revealer of God.

5. Too often we read the Bible merely to learn lessons from its good or bad examples. The Bible does contain various examples of human behavior, but primarily it is a book about God. Discuss some of the things that Jesus the revealer of God teaches us about God from the fourth Gospel.

9

Portraits of Jesus' Person (2)

In the previous chapter we entered John's gallery and viewed his portraits of Jesus as the Christ, Savior, and revealer of God. In this chapter we continue our tour through the gallery to see Jesus as Son of God, life-giver, and Son of man.

The Son of God

John's fourth picture of Jesus portrays him as the incarnate Son of God. Since Jesus possesses and displays divine glory (1:14), it does not surprise us that John the Baptist (1:34) and Nathanael (1:49) testify to his being the Son of God.

The Meaning of "Son of God"

What does Jesus mean when he calls himself the Son of God? John 5:17-18 answers this question. After healing a man who had been lame for thirty-eight years (5:1-9), Jesus teaches publicly that he is the giver of eternal life (5:19-30). The Jewish leaders already opposed him for healing the lame man on the Sabbath. Now they are furious with him because "he was even calling God his own Father, making himself equal with God" (v. 18). By calling God his Father Jesus claims divine equality with him. Thus when Jesus says he is God's Son, he claims to be equal with God.

Moreover, Jesus puts his healing of the lame man on the same level as the supernatural working of God. "My Father is always at his work to this very day [God does not take the sabbath off], and I, too, am working" (v. 17). Jesus is thus the divine Son of God the Father.

John gives many proofs of Jesus' deity. Consider three more from John 5. Since we cannot honor God the Father without honoring his Son, it is God's plan that we honor Jesus as we honor the Father (v. 23). God wants us to worship his divine Son. Furthermore, the Son does something only God can do—he gives eternal life to whomever he wishes (v. 21). In addition, the Son alone has intimate knowledge on earth of what the Father is doing in heaven (v. 19). In sum, Jesus' divine sonship is proved in 5:19-23 by his being (1) the object of worship, (2) the giver of spiritual life, and (3) the sharer of God's secrets.

Glory to the Son of God

Jesus, the Son of God, is glorified by the miracles he performs. By specific comments at Jesus' first and seventh miracles, the apostle John teaches us that Jesus reveals his glory in all the signs. After Jesus' first miracle John reports: "This, the first of his miraculous signs, Jesus performed in Cana of Galilee. He thus revealed his glory, and his disciples put their faith in him" (2:11).

Before going to Bethany to raise Lazarus (the seventh sign), Jesus says that Lazarus's death was "for God's glory so that God's Son may be glorified through it" (11:4). And just before he calls Lazarus from the grave, he says, "Did I not tell you that if you believed, you would see the glory of God?" (11:40). Therefore, Jesus the Son of God reveals his divine glory by doing his signs and thereby brings glory to the Father and to himself.

The Proper Object of Faith

In John 11 Martha, the sister of Mary and Lazarus, makes an important confession concerning Jesus. Jesus has just said to her, "I am the resurrection and the life. He who believes in me will live, even though he dies; and whoever lives and believes in me will never die. Do you believe this?" (11:25-26). Martha replies, "Yes, Lord, I believe that you are the Christ, the Son of God, who was to come into the world" (11:27). When Martha thus confesses that Jesus is the Christ and the Son of God, John illustrates that the chief purpose of the Gospel (as given in 20:30-31) is fulfilled in her life. May God help us realize that Jesus, the Son of God, is the proper object of our faith too.

Executed for Claiming to Be the Son of God

At Jesus' trial before Pilate, three times the governor tells the Jews that he finds no basis for a charge against Jesus (18:38; 19:4, 6). However, the Jews persist in their desire to kill Jesus. "We have a law, and according to that law he must die, because he claimed to be the Son of God" (19:17). There is great irony here. Although the Jewish leaders appeal to their law to accuse Jesus of blasphemy, that same law is one of the prime witnesses to him (5:39-40, 45-47). But the Pharisees and chief priests miss the point of the law and oppose Jesus, God's Son, to the point of crying out for his crucifixion.

For ten years Bernie and Alice Colmar had been faithful members of the so-called Jehovah's Witnesses. They studied every Friday evening at the Kingdom Hall, knocked on many doors to win converts, attended the mass rallies, and pored over the *New World Translation* of the Bible.

Then they met Charlie West, a seminary student, and his wife Phyllis. Bernie and Alice were impressed with the West's concern for them. "I think they really care," Alice remarked to Bernie while they were driving home after an evening with the Wests.

"I agree," admitted Bernie, "but let's not forget that they are not Jehovah's Witnesses. Unless they accept the true faith, they will be annihilated with the rest of the unbelievers."

In time, however, Phyllis challenged the Colmars to study every passage in the New Testament that spoke of Jesus as the Son of God. The two couples agreed to use both of their Bible translations. Slowly God used the love of the Wests and the power of his Word to convince Bernie and Alice that they had an incorrect understanding of Jesus.

"How many years did I repeat the meaningless phrase, 'Jesus is not God, but the Son of God'?" Bernie lamented one evening before his wife and the Wests. "Of course he is not God the Father. He is God the Son—different from, yet equal to, the Father," he said.

"How many people did we mislead?" Alice wondered aloud.

"What can we do?" the Colmars asked the Wests.

"Confess your sins to God and trust his Son as your Savior," Charlie said. "Only Jesus the Son of God is able to save you from your sins." Bernie and Alice did just that, and for the first time in their lives they knew the forgiveness of sins by trusting in Jesus, the Son of God.

Perhaps you have friends trapped in a cult. If you really care, pray for them and study diligently so you can help them to see from the Scriptures that only Jesus, God's Son, can save us from our sins. You may want to consider taking some evening classes in a nearby Bible-believing college or seminary to help you reach out to them.

The Life-Giver

Creator

John's fifth portrait—picturing Jesus as the giver of eternal life—is introduced in the prologue. There we read of the eternal Word who created all of life; indeed, nothing was made apart from him (1:3). Since he gave created life to all things before his incarnation, it is not surprising that as the incarnate Word he gives eternal life to all believers. "Yet to all who received him, to those who believed in his name, he [Jesus] gave the right to become children of God" (v. 12).

The "I Am" Sayings

Many of Jesus' "I am" sayings also show him to be the bestower of eternal life. In fact, each of the following does so: Jesus says he is "the living bread" (6:35), "the good shepherd" (10:11, 28), "the resurrection and the life" (11:25), "the life" (14:6), and "the true vine" (15:1). (For explanations of these sayings see pp. 31-33.)

The Signs

The following signs likewise show that Jesus gives eternal life to

"You believe because I told you I saw you under the fig tree. You shall see greater things than that. . . . you shall see heaven open, and the angels of God ascending and descending on the Son of Man."

The background for this difficult verse is Jacob's dream of the ladder in Genesis 28:12-13. "He had a dream in which he saw a stairway resting on the earth, with its top reaching to heaven, and the angels of God were ascending and descending on it. There above it stood the Lord. . . ." Now it is Jesus, the Son of man, who takes the place of the ladder in Jacob's dream; he connects heaven and earth. Therefore, John 1:51 teaches that Jesus is the mediator between God and men.

The Son of Man Lifted Up

The Son of man who came from heaven must be "lifted up" (John 3:13-15). This lifting up speaks of Jesus' crucifixion (see 12:32-33) and of his return to the Father. In fact, this is an example of John's use of double meaning—Jesus was lifted up both in his crucifixion and in his ascension. John 3:13-15 thus presents a cycle in which Jesus, the Son of man, came down from heaven and will return there.

The Son of Man and Daniel 7

An important background passage for John's references to Jesus as Son of man is Daniel 7:13-14.

> In my vision at night I looked, and there before me was one like a son of man, coming with the clouds of heaven. He approached the Ancient of Days and was led into his presence. He was given authority, glory and sovereign power; all peoples, nations and men of every language worshiped him. His dominion is an everlasting dominion that will not pass away, and his kingdom is one that will never be destroyed.

Jesus expands the concept of the Son of man's "coming on the clouds of heaven" (Dan. 7:13) in the light of his own ministry. When he speaks of the Son of man ascending to where he was before (John 6:62), he is referring to his having come from the Father and returning to the Father. Here again we encounter the cycle of descent and ascent.

Daniel 7:26-27 speaks of the court in session with God ("the Ancient of Days") acting as judge. The judge takes away the authority of the enemies of God so that he and his people will rule forever. Since in John 5 Jesus takes the role that God played in the heavenly courtroom scene of Daniel 7, he is the final judge of the righteous and the wicked (John 5:28-29). "And he [God the Father] has given him [Jesus] authority to judge because he is the Son of Man" (5:27).

The Source of Eternal Life

In his bread of life discourse Jesus says that no one will gain eternal life unless he eats the flesh and drinks the blood of the Son of man—that is, unless he believes in him (John 6:53). Therefore, the Son of man is the source of eternal life; he "is the bread that comes down from heaven, which a man may eat and not die" (v. 50). It is no wonder, then, that God places his seal of approval on Jesus, the Son of man (6:27).

The Jews Will Lift Him Up

The Jewish leaders will lift up Jesus, the Son of man, by killing him. In so doing they will realize who he is and that he truly spoke for God (8:28). This difficult text does not mean that the Jewish leaders will believe in Jesus, but that they will realize they have erred in murdering him. Moreover, it does not mean that they will repent. Instead, they will be all the more hardened in their unbelief. Even after realizing the enormity of their crime, they will persist in rejecting the Son of man.

The Object of Worship

Daniel 7:14 spoke of all peoples worshiping the Son of man. Since

Jesus, the heavenly Son of man, came to earth in fulfillment of Daniel 7, it is therefore proper to direct worship to him. Let us follow the example of the blind man who believed in Jesus as the Son of man and worshiped him (John 9:35-38).

The seventeenth-century hymn "Fairest Lord Jesus," first written in German, captures the desires of our believing hearts:

> Fairest Lord Jesus! Ruler of all nature,
>   O Thou of God and man the Son!
> Thee will I cherish, Thee will I honor,
>   Thou my soul's Glory, Joy, and Crown!
>
> Fair are the meadows, Fairer still the woodlands,
>   Robed in the blooming garb of spring:
> Jesus is fairer, Jesus is purer,
>   Who makes the woeful heart to sing.
>
> Fair is the sunshine, Fairer still the moonlight,
>   And all the twinkling starry host:
> Jesus shines brighter, Jesus shines purer,
>   Than all the angels heaven can boast.
>
> Beautiful Saviour! Lord of the nations!
>   Son of God and Son of Man!
> Glory and honor, praise, adoration,
>   Now and forevermore be Thine!

Review Questions

1. From John 5:17-18 explain what Jesus means when he calls himself "the Son of God."

2. How do we know that the Son of God is glorified by performing miracles?

3. Why was Jesus executed? What is ironic about this?

4. Which signs and "I am" sayings show Jesus to be the giver of eternal life?

5. Explain John 1:51 in the light of its Old Testament background.

Discussion Questions

1. List some proofs of Jesus' deity from John 5. How should the fact that Jesus is God affect our worship? Our faith? Our confidence of salvation? Our witness?

2. The cults hold many incorrect doctrines. Their damning error, however, involves the person of Christ. What is this error, and why is it damning?

3. Why does John teach that the preincarnate Word created all of life in chapter 1 before he recounts Jesus' sermons and signs in the rest of the Gospel?

4. What difference should the fact that Jesus is the life-giver make in our evangelistic strategies and methods?

5. Talk about the meaning of Daniel 7:13-14 in the light of John's presentation of Jesus as Son of man.

10

The Saving Work of Jesus (1)

The television show "To Tell the Truth" was a favorite for many years because of the way it engaged its viewers. A panel of celebrities would question three contestants, all of whom claimed to be the same individual, introduced by that person's name and occupation. The challenge for the panelists, and viewers, was to distinguish the contestant who told the truth from two well-prepared impostors. As the panelists wrote down their choices, we onlookers made up our minds as well. Often we were surprised to find that contestant number two was the right one when we were sure it was number three, and our second choice was number one!

In the preceding two chapters we studied Jesus' person; this chapter and the next will investigate his *work*. Like "To Tell the Truth," John engages his audience in this investigation. However, unlike that TV show, John's Gospel does not leave us guessing. Instead, it openly reveals Jesus' saving work by means of seven themes. Jesus is:

- the Son of man lifted up
- the Good Shepherd
- the Lamb of God
- the priestly sacrifice
- the victor
- the one who would die for the nation
- the grain of wheat that, "dying," bears much fruit

We will cover the first four themes in this chapter and the remaining three in the next.

The Son of Man Lifted Up

Christ's death is presented in the fourth Gospel against the background of Moses' act of lifting up the bronze serpent in the wilderness (3:11-15). In Numbers 21, God sent venomous snakes among the Israelites to punish them for speaking against him and his servant Moses (vv. 4-6). After the people repented, however, Moses prayed to the Lord for them. In obedience to God's instructions, Moses then made a bronze snake and put it on a pole. "Then when anyone was bitten by a snake and looked at the bronze snake, he lived" (v. 9).

God not only gives verbal predictions of the Messiah in the Old Testament; he also makes predictions in actions called *types.* Moses' lifting up the pole in the wilderness is a type of the crucifixion of Christ, as John 3:14-15 reveals. "Just as Moses lifted up the snake in the desert, so the Son of Man must be lifted up, that everyone who believes in him may have eternal life." John 3:18 warns us that all who have not trusted Christ for salvation already stand condemned before God—a worse malady than the snake bites of Numbers 21! Here too, however, is a better remedy—the saving death of the Son of man.

Moses raised the bronze serpent, and all who looked to it were delivered from the snakes. Similarly, Jesus was to be raised up in crucifixion so that all who look to him would be delivered from eternal condemnation. Later, Jesus says, "But I, when I am lifted up from the earth, will draw all men to myself" (John 12:32). The next verse explains Jesus' statement. "He said this to show the kind of death he was going to die." Therefore, Jesus' "being lifted up" refers to his death by crucifixion.

Moreover, "lifted up" is an example of John's using words with double meaning. Jesus is lifted up in crucifixion and also in the sense of being exalted. In fact, the fourth Gospel views the crucifixion as the beginning of Jesus' exaltation (see John 12:23, 27-28; 13:31-32), the first step in his return to the Father.

The double meaning of Jesus' being "lifted up" may have its source in Isaiah 52:13-15. In that passage God says that his servant "will be raised and lifted up and highly exalted" (v. 13). Furthermore, the verses that follow speak of the Messiah's great suffering even unto death. Therefore, Isaiah 52:13–53:12 may lie behind the picture of Jesus being lifted up in death and glory in John's Gospel.

Jesus also speaks of the effects of his death. "I, when I am lifted up from the earth, will draw all men to myself" (John 12:32). The drawing here is the same as that spoken of in 6:44. "No one can come to me unless the Father who sent me draws him, and I will raise him up at the last day." Moreover, the drawing of 6:44 is effective—those drawn do not fail to come to Christ. Therefore, in 12:32 those whom Jesus draws to himself will be saved.

Since the drawing is effective and Jesus said he would draw "all men" to himself, does that mean that *every* person will be redeemed? No, neither here nor elsewhere does the Bible teach *universalism* (the idea that all people will ultimately be saved). Instead, Jesus' statement about "all men" is his response to the Greeks who asked to see him in 12:20-22. Jesus seemed to ignore their request at that time. In fact, instead of agreeing to see the Greeks, he began a discussion of his death. Now by saying "all" he includes the Greeks in the effect of his saving work. Consequently, his crucifixion will deliver not only believing Jews, but believing Gentiles as well.

Ironically, the Jewish leaders inadvertently fulfill Jesus' prediction that he would die by crucifixion. Although Pilate told the Jews to take Jesus and execute him, they protest that they do not have the right to inflict capital punishment. John's inspired comment reads, "This happened so that the words Jesus had spoken indicating the kind of death he was going to die would be fulfilled" (18:31-32). The Jews, of course, put people to death not by crucifixion but by stoning, as the example of Stephen shows (Acts 7:57-60). Crucifixion was the Roman method of execution. So when the Jews refused to put Jesus to death themselves and insisted that Pilate execute him, they were unintentionally fulfilling Jesus' prediction of 12:32.

"At Least 14 Hurt in Pamplona Run," the newspaper headline read. The injured were among the estimated fifteen hundred who ran with the bulls from the corrals to the bullring on the sixth day of the annual week-long San Fermin festival in Spain. The people ran in front of, alongside, and behind the six bulls for the three minutes it took them to complete their course. Since the festival began in

1591, bulls have gored fifty-two runners to death.

How foolish to expose oneself to bodily injury, even death, by "running with the bulls." Yet it is even more foolish to expose oneself to the eternal judgment of God. Still, many people go through life thinking only of the moment, forgetting that they will someday stand before God's judgment seat. Dear reader, do not put off making things right between yourself and God. Jesus, the Son of man was lifted up on the cross to rescue sinners like you. Believe that he died in your place, and you need not fear eternal condemnation.

The Good Shepherd

Jesus says, "I am the good shepherd. The good shepherd lays down his life for the sheep" (10:11). A few verses later, he speaks again of dying in the place of his people (v. 15). Moreover, he willingly dies for them. "No one takes it [my life] from me, but I lay it down of my own accord" (v. 18). He thus voluntarily obeys God the Father by going to the cross. Because of that, the Father loves him all the more (vv. 17-18).

Furthermore, Jesus' death is not the end; it is followed by his resurrection. Actually, his death and resurrection are inseparable, just as he says, ". . . I lay down my life—only to take it up again" (10:17). Again in verse 18, "I have authority to lay it down and authority to take it up again." Since Jesus obeys the Father in laying down his life and in taking it up again, his death and resurrection are according to God's plan. In passing, we notice that here (as in 2:19-22) Jesus speaks of raising himself from the dead. There is only one conclusion: Jesus is divine.

Jesus, the Good Shepherd, gives eternal life to his people, and this gift of eternal life makes believers secure: "I give them eternal life, and they shall never perish"(10:28). Indeed, Jesus emphatically declares that his sheep will never suffer condemnation.

In fact, it is both the Father and the Son who protect the sheep. "No one can snatch them out of my hand. My Father, who has given them to me, is greater than all; no one can snatch them out of my Father's hand. I and the Father are one" (vv. 28-30). How secure are Jesus' sheep! They are kept safe by the power of the Father and the

Son. Jesus' words "I and the Father are one" have often been taken out of context. They mean that Jesus and the Father are one *in their ability to keep the people of God saved.* Of course, this also implies that Jesus is equal with God the Father since only God performs the work of salvation.

Jesus is the Good Shepherd who dies and raises himself to rescue his sheep (notice how Jesus says that his opponents are not his sheep in v. 26). Jesus gives eternal life to his people, and they will be saved forever.

Belshazzar was king of Babylon, the greatest nation on earth. Being a descendant of the great Nebuchadnezzar, he thought that his kingdom would never be overthrown. He felt so secure that he taunted the gods of the peoples Babylon had conquered. After all, the gods of Babylon must be stronger to have defeated their enemies' gods.

Belshazzar held a feast for a thousand of his nobles. They drank wine from the gold and silver goblets that Nebuchadnezzar had taken from the temple in Jerusalem. As they drank they praised their idols and defied the God of Israel (Dan. 5:1-4).

Suddenly, handwriting appeared on the wall in the royal palace; Belshazzar shook with fear as he called for someone to interpret it for him. Brought before the king, Daniel explained the meaning of the mysterious handwriting.

The prophet first recounted the history of God's dealings with Nebuchadnezzar. Then he said:

> But you his son, O Belshazzar, have not humbled yourself, though you knew all this. Instead, you have set yourself up against the Lord of heaven. You had the goblets from his temple brought to you, and you and your nobles, your wives and your concubines drank wine from them. You praised the gods of silver and gold, of bronze, iron, wood and stone, which cannot see or hear or understand. But you did not honor the God who holds in his hand your life and all your ways. Therefore he sent the hand that wrote the inscription (Dan. 5:22-24).

Next, Daniel interpreted the inscription for Belshazzar. "God has numbered the days of your reign and brought it to an end. You have been weighed on the scales and found wanting. Your kingdom is divided and given to the Medes and Persians" (Dan. 5:26-28).

God had spoken through Daniel his prophet and predicted the demise of the wicked Belshazzar. All of the king's imagined security was to no avail, because "that very night Belshazzar, king of the Babylonians, was slain, and Darius the Mede took over the kingdom, at the age of sixty-two" (Dan. 5:30).

No amount of wealth, power, or prestige can provide lasting security. Only the Good Shepherd's sheep know true safety. And the shepherd wants his sheep to enjoy his protection, as the following incident in the life of Pastor Samuel Harris of New Haven, Connecticut, illustrates.

During a fierce storm on December 5, 1871, Pastor Harris, who was delivering a series of lectures at Boston Theological Seminary that week, sat in his room at the Marlborough Hotel in Boston, writing. Being at a loss for a word, he clasped his hands together behind his head and leaned back in his chair to meditate. Scarcely had he done so, when a chimney was blown over by the wind, and a mass of brick and mortar crashed through the roof and ceiling, crushing the table on which the pastor had been writing. Except for the position he was in, Pastor Harris would have been instantly killed. Needless to say, he was thankful for the Good Shepherd's protection.

Is Jesus your shepherd? Does your life show it? On what do you base your security? On your job? Your possessions? Your family? Or on the Lord Jesus, the Good Shepherd?

The Lamb of God

John the Baptist sees Jesus and proclaims, "Look, the Lamb of God, who takes away the sin of the world!" (John 1:29, 36). The background for this statement is the Old Testament sacrificial system. Many lambs (and other animals) were slain by the Israelites as sacrificial offerings in obedience to God's instructions. Some have tried to identify John the Baptist's statement about Jesus with a particular Old Testament sacrifice (the Passover lamb is one example). However, the apostle John presents Jesus as the fulfillment and annulment of *all* the Old Testament sacrifices.

Jesus' death "takes away the sins of the world" (1:29), that is, it is an atoning death that brings forgiveness (see 1 John 3:5). Because Jesus died on the cross as the fulfillment of the Old Testament sacrificial system, we can enjoy the forgiveness of our sins. When John the Baptist says Jesus will remove the sins of "the world" he means that Jesus will rescue all believers—Gentiles as well as Jews—from their sins.

Martin Luther well understood the joy that comes from the forgiveness of sins.

> This is the confidence of Christians and the joyousness of our conscience: that through faith our sins become not ours but Christ's, upon whom God laid the sins of us all and who bore our sins (Isa. 53:6). He is the Lamb of God who bears the sins of the world (John 1:29). All the righteousness of Christ, in turn, becomes ours. For He places his hand upon us, and it is well with us; He, the Savior, blessed forever, spreads His garment and covers us. Amen.

May we understand and experience this joy as well!

The Priestly Sacrifice

John 17 is rightly called Jesus' great high priestly prayer. With cross and resurrection in view (17:4-5, 11, 13, 24), Jesus prays to the Father, "For them I sanctify myself, that they too may be truly sanctified" (v. 19). Jesus' death is presented as a priestly sacrifice in the service of God. In the Old Testament both priest and sacrifice had to be set apart as holy to the Lord (sanctified). Here Jesus is both priest and sacrifice.

Jesus' consecration in death is the cause of the consecration of his people, the basis of their holiness. Those for whom Jesus consecrates himself are the ones the Father has given him (17:2, 6, 9, 24). Jesus therefore dies as the great and final sacrifice to perfect his people in holiness.

The following hymn by Isaac Watts helps us bow in thanksgiving to God who teaches us such wonderful truths about our salvation:

Alas! and did my Saviour bleed,
  And did my Sovereign die!
Would he devote that sacred head
  For such a worm as I!

Was it for crimes that I had done
  He groaned upon the tree!
Amazing pity! Grace unknown!
  And love beyond degree!

Well might the sun in darkness hide,
  And shut his glories in,
When Christ, the mighty Maker, died
  For man, the creature's sin.

Thus might I hide my blushing face
  While his dear cross appears;
Dissolve my heart in thankfulness,
  And melt mine eyes in tears.

But drops of grief can ne'er repay
  The debt of love I owe;
Here, Lord, I give myself away,
  'Tis all that I can do.

Review Questions

1. Explain how Moses' lifting up the serpent in the wilderness is a type of the crucifixion of Jesus.

2. How does John show that Jesus' death and resurrection are inseparable?

3. What is the meaning of John 10:30, "I and the Father are one"?

4. How does the Old Testament help us understand John the Baptist's statements in John 1:29, 36?

5. Explain how Jesus is both priest and sacrifice in John 17:19.

Discussion Questions

1. Does John 12:32 teach universalism? If not, what does it teach? How would your life change if universalism were true?

2. Why do you think the Gospel of John presents Jesus as raising himself from the dead in 2:19-22 and 10:17-18?

3. Show how John 10 teaches the eternal security of believers. What difference should this doctrine make in our lives?

4. Jesus the Lamb of God died an atoning death. Why was atonement necessary? How does Jesus' death atone? What does this mean for you and me?

5. Identify those for whom Jesus consecrates himself in John 17:19.

11

The Saving Work of Jesus (2)

Having surveyed four of John's themes of Christ's saving work in the previous chapter, we are ready to look at the remaining three—Jesus is the victor, the one who would die for the nation, and the grain of wheat that, "dying," bears much fruit.

The Victor

Many Bible students are surprised to learn that the fourth Gospel does not record even one case of Jesus casting out demons. The reason? John does not report the minor conflicts. Instead he focuses his readers' attention on the larger battle between Christ and Satan. After reading that the appointed time has come for Jesus to return to the Father, we learn that the devil puts the idea of betraying Christ into the heart of Judas Iscariot (13:1-2). Thus the idea to betray Jesus is satanic in origin.

In addition, the devil actually empowers Judas to commit the foul deed. In response to John's request to know the identity of the betrayer, Jesus says that he is the one to whom he will give a piece of bread. Our Lord then dips the bread into the sauce and gives it to Judas. "As soon as Judas took the bread, Satan entered into him." Jesus then tells the betrayer to do his evil work quickly (13:27).

It is striking in this context to learn that God has everything in control. "Jesus knew that the Father had put all things under his power, and that he had come from God and was returning to God" (13:3). In fact, Jesus actually teaches that Judas's betrayal is in fulfillment of Psalm 41:9 (John 13:18). God is not the author of sin; Satan and Judas are guilty of the murder of Jesus. Nevertheless, not even this act is out of God's sovereign control.

After predicting his death, resurrection, and ascension to strengthen the faith of his disciples (14:28-29), Jesus says: "I will not speak with you much longer, for the prince of this world [the devil] is coming. He has no hold on me, but the world must learn that I love the Father and that I do exactly what my Father has commanded me" (14:30-31). The devil is coming to slay Christ. Although the devil has no authority over him, Jesus submits to death out of obedience to God the Father. In this way, Jesus shows the world his obedient love for the Father.

Furthermore, Jesus says that the Holy Spirit will come and convict the world concerning its sin, its self-righteousness, and its faulty evaluation of reality (16:8-11). The Spirit will convict the world of its faulty judgment "because the prince of this world now stands condemned" (16:11). The devil has been defeated. Although this passage does not tell us how he is defeated, we conclude from the Gospel of John as a whole that Jesus defeated him at the cross.

The battle lines have been drawn. After Satan gives Judas the idea of betraying Christ, he enters into him and energizes him for his evil deed. Jesus himself speaks of Satan coming to kill him.

Having repeatedly spoken of his impending death (12:23-24, 27-28), Jesus says, "Now is the time for judgment on this world; now the prince of this world will be driven out" (12:31). Jesus' death will result in the overthrow of the world system hostile to God. This agrees with Jesus' statement in 16:33, "I have overcome the world." Moreover, since Satan falsely took authority to himself, he, the ringleader of the evil world system ("the prince of this world"), will be overthrown. Jesus is the mighty victor who defeats the devil and the world!

"I feel so trapped. My life is a wreck. I might as well be dead," Alice moaned as she lay on a bed in the drug rehabilitation center. Alice was sixteen when she ran away from home. Now at the age of twenty-one she despaired of living and was contemplating suicide.

Her life during the past five years had been a living nightmare. She had indeed been trapped—going from one form of bondage to another. To find food and shelter she had become involved with a man who promised to be a father to her. Her "father" turned out to be a pimp who forced her into prostitution. She soon lost her sense of self-worth and began to drink heavily. When she became an alcoholic, the pimp threw her out onto the street since she was no longer of any value to him.

At the suggestion of a fellow street-person Alice went to a rescue mission for a free bed and meal. She sat through many sermons but didn't pay much attention. However, realizing that alcohol was destroying her, she stopped drinking.

After moving to another city, she got a job in a shoe store, where she met a man named Jimmy, whom she began living with. He introduced her to drugs, and soon she was as hooked as he was. She felt free when she was high on heroin and was convinced that she was in control of her life. Then one morning she awoke to find Jimmy dead from a drug overdose. Terrified, she realized that she was in bondage to drugs.

That was when Alice went to the drug rehab center. There during the long days and longer nights filled with sobbing and despair she contemplated suicide as she reflected on the past five years. She had been a slave to one thing after another: men's lust, alcohol, and drugs.

Despite feeling worthless and wanting to die, Alice somehow kept going. Following her release from the drug center she was drawn again to a local rescue mission. "I went for food and a place to sleep. I also went because the other mission was the only place I had been in the past five years where I sensed that people cared about me."

This time Alice listened to the sermons. The message that God loved her filled a void in the center of her life. The words about Christ the victor who delivered sinners from bondage were right on target. "The sermons about Jesus, the mighty champion who would free me from bondage, were like arrows shot right into my heart," she later said. "I wept with joy when I learned that Jesus loved me and gave himself for me."

Today Alice is free. She works at the rescue mission where she came to know Jesus. And she loves to tell others of the freedom she found in Christ.

If you are reading this chapter and find yourself in bondage, in love I point you to Jesus, the mighty victor, who alone is able to deliver you. You may need professional counseling; go to someone who knows and loves the Lord Jesus and who uses the Word of God to help people. May God be gracious to you.

The One Who Would Die for the Nation

After Jesus raises Lazarus, some put their faith in Jesus, but others go and tell the Jewish leaders in Jerusalem what he has done (11:45-46). In response the Jewish authorities call a meeting of the Sanhedrin (the ruling council) to discuss Jesus' ministry. They lament that he is performing so many miracles and influencing so many people. Moreover, they fear that he will bring about a popular uprising within Israel that will lead to intervention by the Romans. Most of all, they fear that as a result the Romans might take away the temple and destroy the nation of Israel (vv. 47-48).

In the midst of this discussion, "Caiaphas, who was high priest that year," informs his colleagues that they do not know what they are talking about. "It is better for you that one man die for the people than that the whole nation perish," he says (v. 50). In this statement of political expediency Caiaphas counsels the rulers to get rid of Jesus in order to avoid the potential disasters they fear.

Since God uses the wrath of men to praise him, John 11:51 reads, "He did not say this on his own, but as high priest that year he prophesied that Jesus would die for the Jewish nation." John is not denying that Caiaphas is guilty of plotting Jesus' death. Instead, he is showing that God uses Caiaphas's evil remarks to predict the atoning death of his Son. Because it is God's plan for the high priest that fateful year to make such a prediction, he causes the high priest to speak in such a way that his words have a double meaning.

In addition, Caiaphas predicts that Jesus will die "not only for that nation [Israel] but also for the scattered children of God, to bring them together and make them one" (11:52). Amazingly, God predicts through the evil high priest that Jesus will die for Jews and Gentiles to bring them together into one church of God! Furthermore, Jesus' death will be substitutionary; he is to die *for* the nation of Israel and *for* all the chosen Gentiles.

Not only does Caiaphas make that prophecy unknowingly, but

his statement serves to strengthen the resolve of the Jewish leaders to kill Jesus. "So from that day on they plotted to take his life" (11:53). Thus the high priest's words help incite the Jews to fulfill the prediction that Messiah would die. This passage well illustrates John's use of irony. How unexpected that Caiaphas, the enemy of Jesus, should predict the atoning death of the Lord!

Thomas O. Chisholm's hymn (based on Isaiah 53) expresses beautifully Jesus' death as our substitute.

> He was wounded for our transgressions,
> He bore our sins in His body on the tree;
> For our guilt He gave us peace,
> From our bondage gave release,
> And with His stripes our souls are healed.
>
> He was numbered among transgressors,
> We did esteem Him forsaken by His God;
> As our sacrifice He died,
> That the law be satisfied,
> And all our sin was laid on Him.
>
> We had wandered, we all had wandered
> Far from the fold of "the Shepherd of the sheep;"
> But He sought us where we were,
> On the mountains bleak and bare,
> And brought us safely home to God.
>
> Who can number His generation?
> Who shall declare all the triumphs of His cross?
> Millions, dead, now live again,
> Myriads follow in His train!
> Victorious Lord and coming King!

The Grain of Wheat That, "Dying," Bears Much Fruit

Some Greeks who have come to Jerusalem for the Passover celebration want to see Jesus (12:20-22). When Andrew and Philip inform him of their desire, he seems to ignore the Greeks, for he says that the hour has come for him to be glorified (v. 23). This, of course, is the appointed time (the "hour") of his death, resurrection, and ascension.

Jesus then tells a little parable: "I tell you the truth, unless a kernel of wheat falls to the ground and dies, it remains only a single seed. But if it dies, it produces many seeds" (v.24). If grain is not planted, it does not reproduce. However, grain sown in the soil bears much fruit. It "dies" because it is buried into the ground and is no longer a grain when it sprouts. Speaking of himself, our Lord teaches that he is the grain of wheat that falls to the ground and dies. Indeed, he is about to die on the cross.

The parable teaches us that Jesus' death will bear fruit—it will issue forth in life for others. Comparing it with the saying in 4:36, we learn that the fruit of the harvest consists of people who are coming to Jesus. Therefore, John 12:24 is an indirect answer to the request of the Greeks in verses 20-22. Since Jesus' death on the cross would be a saving death, it would result in new life for believers—Greeks included.

Next, Jesus applies the parable to his disciples. "The man who loves his life will lose it, while the man who hates his life in this world will keep it for eternal life" (v. 25). Even as Jesus was to lay down his life to bring eternal life to others, so his followers have to "hate" their lives (that is, lose them in his service) in order to be eternally blessed. If they "love" their lives (by living selfishly), they will forfeit them—they will be worth little in terms of eternal values.

The parable of the grain of wheat thus does double duty. It tells of Jesus' dying to save others, and it reminds his followers that they must be ready to die to themselves to serve him.

The remarkable story of Steven Callahan is told in *Reader's Digest* magazine, January 1983. On the last leg of his round-trip crossing of the Atlantic Ocean in his twenty-two-foot sloop *Napoleon Solo,* Steven felt a tremendous crash against the hull. A whale had smashed his boat, and it started to sink. Somehow Steven managed to free his survival duffel and cut loose the life raft. Thus began a seventy-six-day ordeal at sea. Remarkably, Steven survived because of his knowledge of the sea, a determination to see his family again, and the presence of dorados—the fish he grew to love.

On his second day Steven's raft was surrounded by dorados. Their unexpected appearance encouraged him, since they represented life, food, and even companionship. The dorados stayed with the raft, and on the tenth day adrift Steven used his spear gun to kill one. He feasted on the delicious meat, grateful that through the fish's death he might prolong his life. Every few days he would spear another dorado for food.

When the rubber band that released the spear broke, Steven tied the spear to the gun and used it as a hand-held weapon. He was deeply moved when the dorados came closer, as if permitting the weary sailor to take their lives so he could survive.

Callahan had not been a religious man before his adventure, but recognizing God's hand in his survival he began to pray. At one point, however, he was about to give up. Badly in need of food, he lacked the strength to kill the dorados that swam near the bow of his raft. To his amazement one of the fish came alongside and rolled over on its back, exposing its soft underbelly and enabling him to kill it easily.

On April 21, 1982, his seventy-sixth day at sea, Steven Callahan was rescued by fishermen near Antigua. They had come to that area because the dorados surrounding his raft had attracted birds. To the fishermen the birds meant that fish were nearby. Again the dorados had saved his life! Steven was a happy, thankful man. He will never forget his experience with the dorados that seemed to give their lives so that he might live. "What they did for me," he said, "borders on the miraculous."

What the Son of God did for his people *is* miraculous! He, the Lord of glory, became a human being and laid down his life for them. So that we might enjoy eternal life, Jesus died for us. How thankful we should be that he loved us that much! What else can we do, but give our lives in service to him who loved us and gave himself for us?

Review Questions

1. Why does the Gospel of John omit Jesus' exorcisms?

2. How can studying about Christ the victor help us present the Gospel in a fresh way?

3. What did Caiaphas intend by his statement in John 11:50? What did God intend by the same statement?

4. Who are the "scattered children of God" mentioned in John 11:52?

5. Tell how the parable about the grain of wheat does double duty.

Discussion Questions

1. How does John's account of Judas's betrayal of Jesus help us understand God's sovereignty, human responsibility, and the reality of Satan?

2. In what sense has God already defeated his enemies? In what sense is their defeat still future?

3. What do we mean when we say that Jesus' death is substitutionary? Why is this concept important?

4. What temptations in our culture make it easy for us to "love" our lives "in this world" (John 12:25)?

5. Tell how John's various pictures of Jesus' saving work can make us more grateful to God.

his people: the healing of the boy near death (4:46-54), the healing of the lame man (5:1-9), the feeding of the five thousand (6:1-15), the raising of Lazarus (11:38-44), and above all Jesus' resurrection from the grave. (For explanations see pp. 40-42).

The Life-Giver and Evangelism

"Pop didn't do it and neither will I," Don protested. Don's wife, Annette, wanted him to participate in the birth of their first child, but Don felt uneasy about his part in natural childbirth. "I wouldn't be much help to you," he complained. "I'd probably faint." Being a wise Christian woman, Annette resolved not to nag her husband about the matter. Instead, she prayed fervently.

As she prepared to leave for childbirth classes one evening, Don asked her where she was going. After she told him, he said, "Well, I guess it wouldn't hurt for me to attend the classes." Silently she thanked the Lord.

As Don kept attending birthing classes with his wife, his fears melted away. By the delivery date, he was as excited as Annette. Don cried tears of joy and laughter when the doctor placed his firstborn child, a baby boy, into his arms. "To think that I almost missed this event, this new life!" he said to his wife. "Thank you, Lord," he said aloud.

"Thank you, Lord," echoed Annette.

We too can rejoice at the emergence of new life. If we boldly share the gospel, the Lord Jesus, the giver of eternal life, will work through us to draw unsaved people to himslf. Surely it is our responsibility to witness to the Good News of salvation. Yet we must not suppose that we can make sinners alive to God. Only Jesus can do that (5:21; 10:28).

The Son of Man

John's sixth portrait presents Jesus as the Son of man.

Jacob's Ladder

This idea first appears in 1:51, where Jesus replies to Nathanael,

12

The Holy Spirit

Barry had worked for twenty years as a stagehand for a local theater troupe. One evening the actors and actresses surprised him by calling him out on the stage at the end of the performance. Publicly thanking him for his faithful labors, they presented him with a watch and plaque. For a few moments the one who had always been behind the scenes enjoyed the limelight.

God the Holy Spirit worked behind the scenes in the Old Testament. When the main actor in the drama of salvation, the Lord Jesus, appeared on the stage of history, he drew attention to the Spirit of God in a new way. By talking about the Holy Spirit in connection with himself, Jesus put the spotlight on the Spirit.

Let us look at what John says about the Holy Spirit under the following categories:

- The Holy Spirit given to Jesus.
- The Holy Spirit as the source of life.
- Jesus will baptize the church with the Holy Spirit.
- The Holy Spirit will be sent by the Father and the Son.

The Holy Spirit Given to Jesus

As Messiah and Son of God (1:32-34)

Presenting John the Baptist as Jesus' servant who bears witness to him, the fourth Gospel carefully distinguishes the Baptist from the Christ. Thus the prologue tells us that Jesus was the true light, but concerning John it says that "he himself was not the light; he came only as a witness to the light" (John 1:8).

Moreover, John's ministry of baptizing is for the purpose of revealing Jesus to Israel (1:31). Notice the results of John's baptizing Jesus (vv. 32-34).

> Then John gave this testimony: "I saw the Spirit come down from heaven as a dove and remain on him. I would not have known him, except the one who sent me to baptize with water told me, 'The man on whom you see the Spirit come down and remain is he who will baptize with the Holy Spirit.' I have seen and I testify that this is the Son of God."

Although John's Gospel does not record the baptism of Jesus, it gives us a report of the baptism and of its effect on John the Baptist. God gave John the Baptist a sign: he would see the Holy Spirit descend upon the Messiah. When John sees this happen, he knows that Jesus is the Christ. Furthermore, the Holy Spirit's *remaining* on Jesus symbolizes the Spirit's continual empowering of him to speak the words of God. In addition, according to God's design John's baptizing with water is a picture of Jesus the Messiah's baptizing with the Spirit of God. Faithful to his calling, John testifies that Jesus is the messianic king, the Son of God.

As Revealer of God (3:34)

In chapter 3 John the Baptist again testifies to Jesus. When some of John's disciples are concerned that so many people are following Jesus, John's response is characteristic: he rejoices since this is God's doing. The Baptist repeats his earlier insistence that he is not the Christ, but is sent to prepare the way for him (3:27-28).

John the Baptist then likens the people of God to a bride belonging to Jesus, the groom. Being merely the friend of the bridegroom, however, John serves the groom and shares his joy. When his disciples leave the Baptist to follow Jesus, John's mission of preparing the way for the Christ is complete. Henceforth, Jesus will increase in public importance and John will fade out of the picture (vv. 29-30).

Whereas John the Baptist is from the earth, Jesus is from heaven. John is a mere man, but Jesus is the incarnate Son of God whom the Father sent into the world. Accordingly, John speaks of earthly things; Jesus of heavenly. More specifically, the Son of God testifies to what he has seen and heard in the Father's presence. Since he came from heaven, Jesus deserves the highest place, and John is eager to give him that place (vv. 31-32.).

Although Jesus proclaims on earth the very words that the Father gave him in heaven, most hearers do not believe his message. However, the one who accepts Jesus' words certifies that God is truthful. Indeed, the act of believing Jesus' message is a testimony to God's truthfulness (vv. 32-33). The reason is given in the next three verses:

> For the one whom God has sent speaks the words of God, for God gives the Spirit without limit. The Father loves the Son and has placed everything in his hands. Whoever believes in the Son has eternal life, but whoever rejects the Son will not see life, for God's wrath remains on him (3:34-36).

Jesus, of course, is "the one whom God has sent." Because God has given him the Spirit without measure, he speaks the Father's words. Therefore, the Father's gift of the Spirit enables Jesus to reveal God to believers (v. 34).

Furthermore, God the Father loves his Son and has given him great authority. Because of this, men's destinies will be decided by the way they respond to Jesus' message. While believers gain eternal life, those who reject Jesus will be condemned (vv. 35-36).

"Why did the Lord ever have me study computer programming?" the new convert asks. Mature believers, however, know that God always equips his children for the tasks he prepares for them, whether computer programming or whatever. So it is with the apostle Paul. It was Jewish custom for parents to provide manual training for their sons. Therefore, in God's providence Paul supported himself by tentmaking while serving as a Christian missionary (Acts 18:3).

Moreover, God used Paul's experience of studying under the rabbi Gamaliel (Acts 22:3) to sharpen his mind in preparation for writing the great doctrinal letters of the New Testament.

In fact, God always equips his servants. By abundantly pouring out the Spirit upon his Son, God equips him for his work as Messiah. Perhaps we are uneasy at such a thought, because it seems to make Jesus so human. However, we need not be uneasy with any teaching of Scripture, including the teaching that Jesus is both God and man in one person. We do not guard our Lord's deity by minimizing his human nature. Since Jesus is God, he is *able* to save us, as only God can. Since God became a genuine human being in Jesus Christ, he is able to save *us*—his humanity establishes contact with us. Let us grow in our love for Jesus Christ, the God-Man, who loved us and gave himself for us.

The Holy Spirit as the Source of Life

The New Birth (3:5-8)

Nicodemus, a member of the Jewish ruling council (the Sanhedrin) and an important teacher of Israel, has sought out Jesus at night to speak with him (3:1-2). However, by talking about the necessity of a new birth from God, Jesus surprises Nicodemus. "I tell you the truth, no one can enter the kingdom of God unless he is born of water and spirit" (v. 5). When Jesus speaks of a birth of water and of spirit, he is referring to the cleansing promised by the Old Testament prophets, such as in Ezekiel 36:25. "I will sprinkle clean water on you, and you will be clean; I will cleanse you from all your impurities and from all your idols."

"Being born of the Spirit" (John 3:6) means being born of God (see 1:13). Jesus thus teaches that a person has to be cleansed from his sins by God in order to be saved. Moreover, he compares this divine cleansing to a new beginning in life (a birth). In Ezekiel 36:26-27 the Lord said to Israel:

> I will give you a new heart and put a new spirit in you; I will remove from you your heart of stone and give you a heart of flesh. And I will put my Spirit in you and move you to follow my decrees. . . .

Ezekiel's prediction would be fulfilled in the ministry of Jesus. Since Nicodemus is an important teacher in Israel, Jesus expects him to know this from the Old Testament (John 3:10).

Furthermore, Jesus teaches that only the Holy Spirit can bring about this new birth (John 3:6). Likening the Spirit's activity to that of the wind, our Lord means that he is invisible and is known only by his effects (v. 8). Jesus thus teaches that the Holy Spirit is the source of life for the people of God. They cannot make themselves alive to God. Quite the contrary, only the Spirit of God can perform the cleansing needed to give people new life from above.

"The Spirit Gives Life" (6:63)

Communicating some things that are difficult for the crowds to accept, Jesus says, "No one can come to me unless the Father who sent me draws him . . ." (6:44) and, "Unless you eat the flesh of the Son of Man and drink his blood, you have no life in you" (v. 53).

Offended at these hard sayings, Jesus' would-be disciples grumble. But Jesus does not soften his message on their account. Instead he says: "Does this offend you? What if you see the Son of Man ascend to where he was before!" (vv. 61-62). Holding his hearers responsible for their unbelief, Jesus gives occasion for even greater offense!

Then he says: "The Spirit gives life; the flesh counts for nothing. The words I have spoken to you are spirit and they are life" (v. 63). Blaming his unbelieving followers for thinking on earthly rather than on spiritual things, Jesus teaches that the Holy Spirit is the source of spiritual life. In fact, the human and earthly count for nothing in comparison with spiritual matters.

By claiming that his words are "spirit and life," Jesus means that they are spiritual and life-giving. That is, his words primarily deal with spiritual matters. However, because Jesus' hearers' minds are earthbound, they will not believe his words. Although Jesus bears the life-giving message just as the Father intended, the unbelief of the crowds cuts them off from the life Jesus offers. In fact, his grumbling hearers turn back and resolve to follow him no more (v. 66).

To sum up: in John, chapters 3 and 6, Jesus teaches that the Holy Spirit is the source of life for the people of God. It is he who brings about the new birth promised by the Old Testament prophets (3:6-8). And it is he who grants spiritual life (6:63).

"It doesn't matter what you believe as long as you're sincere. That's what I've always thought. And I'm not about to change now at seventy-five years of age," said old Tom. He had been invited by a friend to a Bible study conducted by a young minister at the retirement home where Tom lived. Although he had listened politely to the young man, all the while he intended to make this the last Bible class he would ever attend. As he shook hands with the minister he uttered the words above.

To Tom's consternation the pastor looked him right in the eye and said, "I dare you to prove that from the Word of God."

Since Tom had never been a man to take a dare lightly, he took up the pastor's challenge. Obtaining a copy of the Bible, he began to read. He was well into the Old Testament by the time the Bible class rolled around the following week. "Good to see you, Tom," the minister remarked.

"Humph," said old Tom, irritated at the young man's joy. "I've taken up your challenge, and I'll prove you wrong yet!"

The minister was pleased. He continued patiently to teach the Word of God to the seniors, and he rejoiced to see some of them come to faith. But old Tom was stubborn; he would not give in easily.

It was after he had read the Bible cover to cover four times that Tom asked to speak with the pastor privately. "Pastor," Tom began, "I'm a stubborn old man, and I don't change my mind quickly. For the past six months I have been comparing everything you teach with the Good Book. I am now convinced that you are correct. Jesus is the Son of God, I am a sinner, and this book shows me the only way to heaven. Would you help me come to know Jesus?" With tears in his eyes the young minister led Tom to Christ. The pastor had seen the Spirit of God work through the Word of God to give life to an old man. What joy he had seeing Tom become a child of God at seventy-five years of age!

Jesus Will Baptize the Church With the Holy Spirit

John's Baptism of Jesus (1:32-33)

"I baptize with water, but among you stands one you do not know. He is the one who comes after me, the thongs of whose sandals I am not worthy to untie" (1:26-27). Putting himself far below Christ, John the Baptist considers himself unworthy to take the place of the lowest slave in relation to Jesus! (See pp. 6-7 for information about the custom of footwashing.)

We noticed earlier in this chapter how God used the signal of the descending dove to reveal Christ's identity to John the Baptist. When John baptized Jesus, he knew that he was the one who would "baptize with the Holy Spirit" (1:33). Furthermore, John's baptism with water prefigured Jesus' mighty work of baptizing the church with the Spirit of God.

"Streams of Living Water" (7:37-39)

Jesus stands up on the last and greatest day of the Feast of Tabernacles and invites people to come to him and drink (7:37). As we become more aware of the customs of this feast, we will better understand Jesus' words.

At dawn on the first seven days of the feast, a ceremony of water-pouring took place. A priest leading a procession drew water from the Pool of Siloam with a golden pitcher and returned to the temple. The water was then poured into a funnel on the west side of the altar as the temple choir sang Psalms 113 to 118 in praise to God. Indeed, the whole ceremony was designed to give thanks to God for his gift of rain the previous year and to ask him to provide in the coming one.

Jesus uses the fact that on the eighth (and last) day of the Feast of Tabernacles there was no ceremony of water-pouring. Thus all attention would be directed toward him who says: "If anyone is thirsty, let him come to me and drink. Whoever believes in me as the Scripture has said, streams of living water will flow from within him" (John 7:37-38).

By claiming to be the one who provides water for the people to drink, Jesus puts himself in the place of God, the giver of rain. Furthermore, the apostle John explains the meaning of this "water" to which Jesus refers. "By this he meant the Spirit, whom those who believed in him were later to receive. Up to that time the Spirit had not been given, since Jesus had not yet been glorified" (v. 39).

Jesus is speaking of the "water" of the Spirit of God that he would pour out upon the church on the day of Pentecost in Acts 2. However, Jesus must first be crucified and then glorified before the Spirit would be given to the church in new fullness and power. As is customary in the Gospel of John, the people have a divided response to Jesus' words (7:40-44).

Jesus Breathes on the Disciples (20:21-22)

When the risen Lord Jesus appears to the disciples (Thomas being absent), they are overjoyed (John 20:19-20). "As the Father has sent me, I am sending you," he says to them (v. 21). Since the Son of God has completed the task for which the Father sent him, he now commissions his disciples to spread the gospel to others. By performing an action he reinforces the meaning of his words. "And with that he breathed on them and said, 'Receive the Holy Spirit. If you forgive anyone his sins, they are forgiven; if you do not forgive them, they are not forgiven' " (vv. 22-23).

Here Jesus symbolically equips his followers for their mission. By breathing on them (the same Greek word means *breath, breathing,* and *spirit* or *Spirit*), he pictures their reception of the Spirit of God for ministry. I understand Jesus' action to be a prediction of his giving of the Spirit to the church on the day of Pentecost. Furthermore, the disciples' forgiving or not forgiving sins refers to their preaching the Gospel empowered by the Holy Spirit.

Thus Jesus symbolically portrays his pouring out of the Spirit of God on the disciples to prepare them for their preaching ministries. As their hearers respond with faith in the message, their sins are forgiven; but those who reject the apostolic gospel will not be forgiven.

The bricklayer carefully put the brick in place, scraped off the excess mortar, and used a level to make sure the wall was proceeding as planned. Meanwhile, some boys who had been playing baseball on a field adjacent to the library where the bricklayer was working took a break between games. At first they watched at a distance as the man laid the bricks. But before long they had drawn closer and were asking him questions.

Seeming not to mind the interruption of his labors, the bricklayer explained to the boys that although the bricks were strong, they needed the mortar to hold them together; bricks piled one on another without mortar could easily be toppled. And although the tub of mortar with which he worked would soon harden into a strong building material, it was not nearly as strong or attractive by itself as when used with the bricks. Therefore, the bricklayer used both bricks and mortar to construct a sturdy, handsome library wall.

Later, my oldest son, one of the ballplayers, told me of the bricklayer's work. What a picture of both the Spirit and the gospel, I thought. Although the gospel is God's powerful message of salvation, it must still be used by the Spirit of God to be effective. And the Spirit doesn't work alone to save sinners. He works through the gospel. Just as bricks and mortar must be combined to build a wall, so the gospel and the Spirit are inseparable in God's plan of salvation.

Let us freely share the Good News, trusting in the power of the Holy Spirit to produce results.

The Holy Spirit Will Be Sent by the Father and the Son

Instructing his disciples concerning the Holy Spirit in his farewell discourses in John 14-16, Jesus refers to him as "the Spirit of Truth," "the Holy Spirit," and most frequently as "the Paraclete." Since there is no one suitable way to translate into English the Greek word *parakletos,* I will use the English form *paraclete* and show its meaning in each passage. Jesus uses the name "Paraclete" to designate the Spirit in his special role as Jesus' representative in the world after his return to the Father.

The Paraclete Will Be With the Disciples as Their Friend (14:16-17)

As Jesus is about to return to the Father, he promises to ask him to send another Paraclete (here and in the next two passages meaning "helper") to be with the disciples forever (14:16). When the Father answers Jesus' prayer, we learn that in his loving-kindness he will send another one like Jesus to be with them—the Spirit of truth. However, because the world only knows what it sees, Jesus says that it cannot accept the Spirit, since it does not see him or know him. In contrast, the disciples will know the Spirit of truth, for he will live with them and indwell them (v. 17).

After the Smithson's housing development had been plagued by a rash of burglaries, Adam Smithson vowed that his family would never become a crime statistic. So he stayed up late on Friday nights—the time the burglar usually struck—in hopes of catching the thief.

Having dozed off at the kitchen table one Friday night, Adam was awakened by the sound of footsteps. Slowly he inched toward the sound. Readying himself to swing a baseball bat at what he thought was the intruder, he recognized the outline of his oldest son in the near darkness. "Johnny!" he cried aloud, "I almost bashed you in the head!" Johnny, who had been sleepwalking, didn't hear a word, and thankfully Adam carried his son upstairs and put him to bed.

Figuring that his thief-hunting was a bad idea, the shaken father was ready to retire when he heard someone at the basement door. Quietly he crept downstairs and positioned himself behind the door at the head of the basement steps. Since he could hear the would-be thief coming up the steps, he crouched in the darkness, and when the door opened, he knocked the intruder unconscious with one blow. Mr. Smithson then called the police, who arrived quickly and arrested the burglar.

Adam Smithson was a friend to his family but an enemy of the robber. In a similar way the Holy Spirit is a friend of Christians and an enemy of the unsaved. Since the Holy Spirit is God, he is everywhere (see Ps. 139:7-10). In this sense the Spirit is as much with the unsaved as he is with Christians. But, since unbelievers do not know or obey the Spirit, he is with them as an alien, an intruder, an enemy. However, when a person comes to know the Lord, the ever-present Spirit becomes a dear friend, a constant companion, a welcome guest.

Christian reader, do you appreciate the presence of the Holy Spirit in your life as you should? Do you rely upon your dear divine friend? Do you commune with your constant companion? Are you thankful for your welcome guest?

The Paraclete Will Teach the Disciples (14:25-26)

John 14:25-26 is similar to the previous passage.

> All this I have spoken while still with you. But the Counselor [Paraclete], the Holy Spirit, whom the Father will send in my name, will teach you all things and remind you of everything I have said to you.

Jesus promises that after his departure the Father will send the Spirit. In addition, Jesus shows the significance of the name "Spirit of truth" (used in 14:17 and 15:26)—it is the Spirit who will deliver the truth. During his earthly ministry Jesus has been the revealer of God to the disciples, but now the Spirit of truth will take over the teaching role. Specifically, the Spirit will remind them of the things Jesus has said, much as the Son of God has spoken on behalf of the Father. "These words you hear are not my own; they belong to the Father who sent me" (14:24). Furthermore, since the Savior knows that his disciples, confused and afraid, cannot fully understand his words, he reassures them by promising them his peace (v. 27).

We can be thankful that Jesus does not leave the responsibility of writing the Gospels to the disciples' memories alone. Instead he promises that the Spirit will remind them of the things Jesus has taught them. I wonder if we American Christians treasure the Word of God as we should. I have read of believers in the Soviet Union staying up all night to copy Scripture portions by hand. How they must highly value God's holy Word! What about us? Although we have many copies of the Bible in our homes, do we take the Scriptures for granted? Or do we hunger for the Word of God and cherish it as our fellow believers in less fortunate circumstances?

The Paraclete and the Disciples Will Testify (15:26-27)

While warning his followers that the world will hate and persecute them even as it did him (in John 15:18–16:4), Jesus speaks again of the Paraclete.

> When the Counselor [Paraclete] comes, whom I will send to you from the Father, the Spirit of truth who goes out from the Father, he will testify about me. And you also must testify, for you have been with me from the beginning (15:26-27).

Aware that the world will hate his disciples, the Savior nevertheless wants them to witness to the world. Moreover, they will not be alone in their witness, for Jesus will equip them by sending them the Paraclete. Therefore, the Spirit of truth *and* the disciples will bear witness to Jesus.

The Paraclete Will Convict the World (16:7-11)

Assuring the disciples that his returning to the Father is good for them, Jesus says, "Unless I go away, the Counselor [Paraclete] will not come to you; but if I go, I will send him to you" (16:7). After he ascends, Jesus will send them the Spirit. Although the word *paraclete* sometimes means "defense attorney" (see 1 John 2:1), in John 16:8-11 Jesus predicts that the Paraclete will function as a prosecuting attorney.

> When he comes, he will convict the world of guilt in regard to sin and righteousness and judgment: in regard to sin because men do not believe in me; in regard to righteousness, because I am going to the Father, where you can see me no longer; and in regard to judgment, because the prince of this world now stands condemned.

Whereas in John 14 and 15 Jesus said that the Spirit would minister to the disciples, now he says that the Spirit will minister to the world. Specifically he will convict the world on three different counts; he will convict the world of its sin, righteousness, and judgment. Although there have been many different interpretations of these verses, I am following that of D. A. Carson who suggests we understand the world as the *doer* of sin, righteousness, and judgment.

First, the Paraclete will convict the world of its sin because people do not believe in Jesus (16:9). Since people do not trust Jesus as Savior on their own, all will perish unless God graciously sends the Spirit to convict them. Therefore, he sends the convicting Spirit precisely *because* people do not believe in his Son. Surely God is good to bring salvation to those who could never find it by themselves!

Second, the Paraclete will convict the world of its righteousness. If the world is the doer of this righteousness, then it must be self-righteousness. So, the Spirit will show the sinful world its self-righteousness. In fact, this is exactly what Jesus has been doing. "The world . . . hates me because I testify that what it does is evil" (7:7; see also 5:39-44; 7:21-24; 8:42-47). Now, since Jesus is going to the Father and will no longer be seen by the disciples, the Spirit will take his place (16:10).

Third, the Paraclete will convict the world of its judgment. If we maintain the symmetry of the passage, the world must be the performer of this judgment. John uses the word *judgment* in two senses: it sometimes means "condemnation" (3:19; 5:24; 12:31) and at other times, "evaluation" (5:30; 7:24; 8:15-16). Here it must mean the world's faulty evaluation of spiritual matters. Therefore, the Spirit will convict the world of its false assessment of spiritual things.

Furthermore, Jesus gives the reason for this third ministry of the Spirit—"because the prince of this world now stands condemned" (16:11). Anticipating going to the cross and doing battle with the devil, Jesus knows that his death will mean defeat for the evil one. In fact, since Jesus has already resolved to die, it is as if Satan were already a defeated foe. Moreover, Satan's defeat signals that the last times are already here, and this gives great urgency to the Spirit's convicting ministry. Since the last days are here, the Spirit will point out to the world its faulty evaluation of spiritual reality. How desperately the world needs to see its need and believe in Jesus!

"Wow, I'm busy for the Lord every night this week!" exclaimed Joseph. Although he had been a Christian for only a month, already he had adopted a new lifestyle. Having been taught by his new Christian friends that a Christian does Christian things with other

Christians, he was quickly caught up in his new round of activities. And he enjoyed his new friends and new way of life.

However, before long a comment by one of his former buddies brought him up short. "Hey, it's holy Joe," he said. "I guess you don't have time for us heathen anymore, eh?" Joseph was wounded by these words. Although he had not intended to turn his back on all his former friends, that is exactly what he had done.

Turning to the New Testament for direction, he read that Jesus was a friend of sinners and that Christians were to be light for a dark world. He winced when he read about people lighting a lamp and putting it under a bowl (Matt. 5:15). "That's just what I have done," he thought. "I have hidden my light from the very people who need it."

After asking God's forgiveness and resolving to do better, Joseph deliberately set aside two evenings a week for involvement with his unsaved friends. He played in a softball league with them as he had for several years. Only this time they saw a difference in his life. Waiting until his friends asked about the changes in his life, he told them about Jesus. And after the Spirit of God convicted two of them, they trusted Christ and are living for him today. "The main reason why the Lord brought me to himself," Joseph concluded from this experience, "is so I can tell others what he has done for me." Joseph has learned the important lesson of spending time with unsaved people to tell them about Christ. Have you? Since the Holy Spirit brings conviction to a needy world through forgiven sinners like you and me, let us get busy for God.

The Paraclete Will Glorify Jesus (16:13-15)

John 16:13-15 completes the teaching of the Gospel of John on the Holy Spirit. After Jesus says that he has more to tell the disciples than they can presently bear, he promises:

> But when he, the Spirit of truth, comes, he will guide you into all truth. He will not speak on his own; he will speak only what he hears, and he will tell you what is yet to come. He will bring glory to me by taking from what is mine and making it known to

you. All that belongs to the Father is mine. That is why I said the Spirit will take from what is mine and make it known to you (16:13-15).

Knowing that the disciples are burdened down and cannot receive any more instruction at this time, Jesus promises that in the future the Spirit of truth will continue Jesus' teaching ministry. Even as Jesus has made the Father known to the disciples, so the Spirit will make the Father and the Son known to them. Since in God's plan the disciples would write the New Testament, he has provided for their ongoing instruction by the Spirit.

Our Lord has wonderfully saved the most important aspect of the Spirit's ministry for last. "He will bring glory to me . . ." (v. 14). Having glorified the Father while on earth (17:4), Jesus is now ready to return to him in heaven. Subsequently, he and the Father will send the Spirit of God to teach the disciples. By making known to the disciples the things that Jesus has taught them, the Spirit will glorify Jesus.

Let us make Bessie P. Head's hymn "O Breath of Life" our prayer.

> O Breath of Life, come sweeping through us,
>   Revive Thy Church with life and pow'r;
> O Breath of Life, come, cleanse, renew us,
>   And fit Thy Church to meet this hour.
>
> O Wind of God, come bend us, break us,
>   Till humbly we confess our need;
> Then in Thy tenderness remake us,
>   Revive, restore, for this we plead.
>
> O Breath of Love, come breathe within us,
>   Renewing thought and will and heart;
> Come, Love of Christ afresh to win us,
>   Revive Thy Church in every part.
>
> O Heart of Christ, once broken for us,
>   'Tis there we find our strength and rest;
> Our broken contrite hearts now solace,
>   And let Thy waiting Church be blest.

Revive us, Lord! Is zeal abating
  While harvest fields are vast and white?
Revive us, Lord, the world is waiting,
  Equip Thy Church to spread the light.

Review Questions

1. What effect did Jesus' baptism have upon John the Baptist?

2. Tell how Ezekiel 36:25-27 helps you understand John 3.

3. What did Jesus mean when he said that his words are "spirit" and "life" (John 6:63)?

4. Why did Jesus breathe on his disciples in John 20:22?

5. How does the convicting ministry of the Paraclete in John 16:8-11 display God's grace?

Discussion Questions

1. How are Jesus' deity *and* his humanity essential for our salvation?

2. Show how a knowledge of the customs of the Feast of Tabernacles can help you understand Jesus' words in John 7:37-38. What tools could you use to learn more about the customs of Bible times?

3. Are we as conscious of the inseparability of the Spirit and the gospel as we should be when we share our faith? If not, how can we improve?

4. Discuss the ways in which the Paraclete takes Jesus' place. How can we better appreciate the Spirit's presence in our lives and his ministries to us?

5. Thanks be to God for fulfilling the promises of John 14:26 and 16:13-14 and giving us the New Testament! How can we treasure God's Word more?

13

The Last Things

We need to look at an object from different vantage points to get the whole picture. Take a mountain, for example. A family on vacation admires its purple majesty from their car window. To them it is the most beautiful sight of the day. A pilot flying overhead looks down and smiles at his gigantic friend, a familiar landmark on his navigational charts. A climber stops to rest on one of its snowy crags. He sees the mountain as a worthy opponent to be conquered. Three pictures: majestic sight, friendly landmark, and worthy foe. And each adds to our understanding of the mountain.

The fourth Gospel teaches us concerning the last things (perhaps you are more familiar with the term *prophecy*) from three different vantage points as well. These are:

- the Old Testament
- the "time" sayings
- fulfilled and unfulfilled prophecy

By studying all three perspectives, we will get a better view of the whole of John's teaching on prophecy.

The Vantage Point of the Old Testament

From the perspective of the Old Testament the coming of the Messiah was future. The fourth Gospel presents Jesus as that promised Messiah (or Christ). Since we have already studied John's picture of Jesus as the Christ (see pp. 75-78), here we only add a few examples and show how Jesus' being the Christ fits with the doctrine of last things.

Jesus and Old Testament Predictions

In almost every chapter of the Gospel of John Jesus appears as the Christ who has come to fulfill the Old Testament. Sometimes Jesus specifically fulfills Old Testament predictions. Such is the case in John 15, where Jesus speaks of the Jewish leaders' great unbelief in the face of his own miracles and messages from God (vv. 22-25):

> If I had not come and spoken to them, they would not be guilty of sin. Now, however, they have no excuse for their sin. He who hates me hates my Father as well. If I had not done among them what no one else did, they would not be guilty of sin. But now they have seen these miracles, and yet they have hated both me and my Father. But this is to fulfill what is written in their Law: "They hated me without reason" [Ps. 69:4].

Contrary to the reader's first impression, Jesus is not denying that the Jewish leaders were sinners before he preached to them. Rather, here is an example of John's use of an exaggerated comparison. Jesus' point is that the Jewish leaders' previous guilt is nothing compared to their guilt in rejecting his words and works. Thus he says in effect, "Woe to you, scribes and Pharisees, for rejecting the supreme revelation of God!" Most important for our immediate purposes, Jesus regards the Jews' rejection of him as fulfilling Psalm 69:4.

Furthermore, Jesus in his triumphal entry fulfills the words of Zechariah 9:9.

> Jesus found a young donkey and sat upon it, as it is written, "Do not be afraid, O Daughter of Zion; see, your king is coming, seated on a donkey's colt" (John 12:14-15).

In addition, Jesus considers his betrayal by Judas as the fulfillment of Psalm 41:9.

> I am not referring to all of you; I know those I have chosen. But this is to fulfill the scripture: "He who shares my bread has lifted up his heel against me" (John 13:18).

Jesus is also presented as the Christ when others do things to him that fulfill Old Testament predictions. To cite one example: the soldiers who crucify Jesus divide up his clothes into four shares, one for each of them; but since his undergarment is seamless, they decide not to tear it to divide it. Instead, they cast lots to see which one of them should get it. Next we read, "This happened that the scripture might be fulfilled which said, 'They divided my garments among them and cast lots for my clothing'" (John 19:23-24 quoting Ps. 22:18). Of course, this does not mean that the soldiers deliberately fulfill the Old Testament. Rather, God uses their selfish actions to carry into effect the predictions of his Word.

Jesus, the Long-awaited One

In the midst of her conversation with Jesus, the Samaritan woman says, "I know that Messiah is coming. When he comes, he will explain everything to us" (4:25). By replying "I who speak to you am he," Jesus claims to be the Christ who was promised in the Old Testament. Later he tells the Jews, "Your father Abraham rejoiced at the thought of seeing my day; he saw it and was glad" (8:56). Looking forward in faith Abraham joyously anticipated the time when God would send the promised one. Jesus is that promised one; he is the Christ.

Reader's Digest once carried a story about a man who suffered amnesia after falling and hitting his head on the way home from work. After a period of unconsciousness, he came to but did not know how to get home. Instead of walking a few blocks to his house, he boarded a bus that took him to a town miles away. Still unable to remember who he was, he took a job washing dishes in a restaurant and reluctantly began a new life.

His wife, of course, had no idea what happened to him. Although she called the police and reported him missing, they were unable to help. An so she began a time of waiting that would last several years. During that time she never lost confidence in her husband.

More than ten years after having left home, the man again hit his head, and amazingly he regained his memory. "I now know who I am! I remember my past!" he excitedly told his co-workers. "I must return to my wife."

That evening, as the man's wife sat reading in their living room, there was a knock on the door. When she opened the door, there stood her long-awaited husband. For a few moments they just stared at each other. Then, they embraced. "It's so good to have you home," she cried.

"It's good to be home," he replied. After more hugs and kisses, he proceeded to tell her his story.

"I didn't know what had happened," she said, "but I knew you were faithful—and I never lost hope."

From the vantage point of the Old Testament Jesus was the long-awaited Christ. Although the prophets foretold the coming of the deliverer, none of them lived to see him. Even the godly remnant of Israel in Old Testament times could only wait in hope that God would honor his promises to the fathers. By sending his Son into the world, God honored those promises and the long time of waiting was over—Jesus the Christ was here! Sometimes we forget that today we live in the most exciting time in the history of the world. Doubtless, it is remarkable what the Old Testament saints like Joseph, Deborah, and David were able to accomplish for God. However, since Jesus has come, how much more should we now honor God in all things!

The Vantage Point of the "Time" Sayings

Since we have already studied the "time" sayings in chapter 6, here we only want to examine their significance for John's doctrine of last things. The "time" sayings help us gain a wide view of Jesus' ministry; that is, they demonstrate that God has a big plan of salvation and that Jesus plays the most important part in that plan.

God's plan of salvation stretches from the earthly ministry of our Lord (4:23; 5:25; 16:25, 29) all the way to the future resurrection of the dead (5:28). In fact, taking all of Scripture into account, God's plan goes from before creation (eternity past) to the new heavens and new earth. Moreover, this plan includes Jesus' triumphal entry into Jerusalem (2:4; 7:6, 8) and the Father's protection of his unique Son (7:30; 8:20). In addition, it embraces the persecution of the disciples (16:2, 4, 32) and the fact that believers no longer have to worship in Jerusalem (4:21, 23).

Above all, however, the plan of God centers in Jesus' appointed time to be crucified, to raise himself from the dead, and to go back to the Father (12:23, 27; 13:1; 17:1). In fact, these are the most important events in the history of the world. Therefore, when we understand their centrality in the plan of God, we can reap many practical benefits.

How Were Old Testament Believers Saved?

Many Christians have questions about the salvation of believers in the Old Testament. Reading Hebrews 11 or Romans 4, they correctly conclude that Old Testament believers were saved. Furthermore, they know that no one was ever saved by works. But they get into difficulty when they try to explain *how* people could be saved by Jesus' death and resurrection when he hadn't yet come.

The answer lies in the fact that the Old Testament looked forward to Christ's coming. In God's plan no one would ever be saved except through Christ's atonement (his death to take away our sins). Since believers in the Old Testament didn't understand the details of Christ's death and resurrection, God held them responsible to believe the truth he had given them. By applying the benefits of the saving work of Christ to Old Testament believers, God forgave their sins with a view to Jesus' bringing salvation at the appointed time.

The New Testament tells of the ultimate effects of Christ's death and resurrection—the final salvation of *all* believers in the presence of God. How thankful we should be that Jesus' appointed time had come!

Thankful Hearts

Today we are bombarded with *hedonism*—the idea that the chief reason for living is the pursuit of happiness. Repeatedly television commercials tell us, "You owe it to yourself," and "real pleasure is found" in using this or that product. Spending hours in front of the TV, many gawk over the lifestyles of the rich and famous. And one reason for soap operas' popularity is that they enable the viewer to enjoy vicariously the pleasures of the characters in the stories without suffering the consequences of their actions.

I know a man, however, who is truly happy despite his lack of great wealth, possessions, or fame. His secret? He has learned the importance of *gratitude*. Greg is thankful for the things in life that most others take for granted: a good wife and children, a tidy house, an appetizing meal, a warm bed, and good health. Most of all, he and his family are thankful for Jesus' coming in the plan of God to rescue them from their sins.

As believers in Christ we must learn to swim against the current of hedonism. Otherwise we will be pulled along with the world into thinking that pleasure is the most important thing. No! The Lord Jesus and his salvation are most important. As we learn daily to be more thankful to Christ for saving us and for the easily overlooked blessings, we will find happiness. For happiness does not come from seeking it; rather, it is a by-product of a thankful heart.

May God enable us every day to live the truth of J. S. Mohler's hymn "With Thankful Hearts, O Lord, We Come."

> With thankful hearts, O Lord, We come,
> To praise Thy name in grateful song;
> Accept the offering, Lord, we bring,
> And help us loud Thy praises sing.
>
> We thank Thee, Lord, for daily food,
> For plenteous store of earthly good;
> For life, and health, we still possess,
> With house and home so richly blest.
>
> We thank Thee for Thy blessed Word,
> That to our souls doth life afford;
> Help us its message to receive,
> And from the heart its truth believe.

The Vantage Point of Fulfilled and Unfulfilled Prophecy

The New Testament doctrine of the future deals with things that are already fulfilled (the "already") and things that are yet to be fulfilled (the "not yet"). Some of the "time" sayings we have studied exhibit a tension between fulfillment ("a time has come") and unfulfillment ("a time is coming"; see pp. 57-59). This tension is expressed in other ways in John's Gospel as well.

Salvation and Judgment

We normally think of God's pronouncement of the final verdicts of salvation and judgment in connection with the last day. Jesus' words in John 12:25 fit well with this point of view. "The man who loves his life will lose it, while the man who hates his life in this world will keep it for eternal life." Since it is used over against "life in this world," "eternal life" here refers to the future glory of believers.

However, the fourth Gospel rarely uses "eternal life" in this future sense. Instead, "eternal life" almost always is portrayed as the present possession of the believer. To cite one example:

> For God did not send his Son into the world to condemn the world, but to save the world through him. Whoever believes in him is not condemned, but whoever does not believe stands condemned already because he has not believed in the name of God's one and only Son (John 3:17-18).

Here the verdicts of salvation and judgment belonging to the last day are announced beforehand. In fact, in the earthly ministry of Jesus we learn what God's sentence will be on that day. Although those who believe in Jesus will not suffer condemnation, unbelievers have been condemned already. It follows, then, that as long as one persists in unbelief, he can be sure that judgment lies ahead. Therefore, in John 3:17-18 we see the perspective of the "already" concerning salvation and judgment.

"I know the meaning of that verse," said Alec, a recently saved and growing Christian. Looking at Alec, the Bible study leader asked him to explain Proverbs 14:12, "There is a way that seems right to a man, but in the end it leads to death."

"I talked to a young man about Christ yesterday," Alec began, "who showed little interest in the things of God. When I asked him if he was going to heaven, he said that when he stood before God to be judged he hoped that his good deeds would outweigh his bad ones."

Nodding heads indicated that others in the group had received similar responses. "That is a good example of the way that seems right to a man but in the end leads to spiritual death," Alec continued. "Contrary to the young man's faulty ideas, if we trust Jesus as our Savior, we can know *now* that we are saved."

"Right, Alec," said the group leader. "Jesus, the judge of the earth, has come ahead of time to announce the verdicts of the last day. So we don't have to wait until death to know our final destiny. We can know it now based upon our relationship to Christ. If we reject him, we are condemned. If we trust him as Savior, we know that we will be saved."

The Resurrection of the Dead

The resurrection of the dead is also both present and future in the Gospel of John. When we studied the "time" sayings, we learned that in the ministry of Jesus, people were spiritually resurrected in passing from death to life. This is the meaning of John 5:24-25, where Jesus says:

> I tell you the truth, whoever hears my word and believes him who sent me has eternal life and will not be condemned; he has crossed over from death to life. I tell you the truth, a time is coming and has now come when the dead will hear the voice of the Son of God and those who hear will live.

These verses attest to the resurrection of the dead in the "already." However, the time is still future when the bodies of the dead will physically rise from the grave according to Jesus' words in John 5:28-29.

> Do not be amazed at this, for a time is coming when all who are in their graves will hear his voice and come out—those who have done good will rise to live, and those who have done evil will rise to be condemned.

Here we read of the "not yet" dimension to the resurrection of the dead. Some Christians are troubled because they think these verses teach salvation by works. Of course, the Bible teaches salvation by grace alone through faith alone in Christ alone. Nevertheless, it also teaches *judgment* based upon the thoughts, words, and deeds of mankind (see also Matt.7:21-23; 25:31-46; Rom. 2:5-11; Rev. 20:11-15). Furthermore, there is no contradiction between justification by faith and judgment based upon deeds. Whereas the evil deeds of unbelievers are the basis of their condemnation, the good works of believers are the fruit of the Holy Spirit and the result of their free justification.

Jesus again refers to the future bodily resurrection of the dead when he says, "And this is the will of him who sent me, that I shall lose none of all that he has given me, but raise them up at the last day" (John 6:39; see also 6:40, 44, 54).

We therefore see present and future dimensions to the resurrection of the dead in the Gospel of John. While believers in Christ are raised spiritually in the "already," the resurrection of the bodies of the just and unjust is "not yet."

In our day some Christian leaders seem to confuse fulfilled and unfulfilled aspects of biblical prophecy. Consider Hobart Freeman, who started a number of churches in the Midwest. He taught that God does not will for Christians to be sick. Prohibiting the use of medicines, he expected believers to trust God instead. The results of his teaching were devastating. Diabetics who failed to take insulin died. Mothers and their babies lost their lives during childbirth. Freeman finally went so far as to announce that he was so full of faith that he would never die! But in 1987 Hobart Freeman passed away.

I wish that with his death the tragedy and bad publicity would have ceased, but lawsuits against Freeman and his churches continue. The old saying is true: Bad doctrine results in bad practice. Although God sometimes heals people today, the time for the salvation of our bodies lies in the future, when God will raise us from the dead and give us glorified bodies. Until Christ returns, we all will experience weakness, illness, and eventually death.

The Second Coming of Christ

The same tension between fulfilled and unfulfilled prophecy exists in John's presentation of the second coming of Christ. Jesus promises his disciples that after he returns to the Father, he will come back and take them to be with him (John 14:3). He also speaks of his second coming at the end of the Gospel when he says to Peter concerning John: "If I want him to remain alive until I return, what is that to you? You must follow me" (21:22). These two passages plainly refer to the future return of Christ.

However, in John 14:23 Jesus speaks of an "already" aspect to his second coming. "If anyone loves me, he will obey my teaching. My Father will love him, and we will come to him and make our home with him." The language here is similar to that of 14:1-3, where Jesus speaks of going to his Father's house with its many rooms to prepare places for his disciples. His point is that the disciples belong to God and will be welcome in his presence. In contrast, in 14:23 Jesus speaks not of coming and taking the disciples to the Father's house; rather he speaks of himself and the Father coming to the believer and making their dwelling place with him. There is therefore a sense in which even the second coming of Christ finds present fulfillment in the warm relationship between the Father and Son and Christians.

The Glorification of Believers

The glorification of believers also reflects the "already" and "not yet" tension. In his famous prayer Jesus prays to the Father, "I want those you have given me to be with me where I am, and to see my glory. The glory you have given me because you loved me before the creation of the world" (John 17:24). Envisioning his cross and resurrection as past events, Jesus here prays that the Father would bring the people of God to heaven to be with Christ and to see his glory. This clearly refers to the future. Yet in verse 22 Jesus says, "I have given them the glory that you gave me, that they may be one as we are one." There is thus also a present dimension to the glorification of the believer.

We have now looked at the mountain from three different vantage points. May our journey not have been in vain. Let us examine our lives so that we do not end up like an unfortunate man I once read about. A wealthy relative in England had passed away and left the man a fortune. Although legal representatives sent letters to him in America informing him of his inheritance, he disregarded them and never responded. Finally, they went to see him in person, but the result was the same. Because the foolish man refused to believe that the great inheritance was his, he died as he had lived—a pauper.

Every Christian is spiritually rich in the promised blessings of heaven. Surely this should make a difference in our daily lives. We are not to live as those who do not know Christ, as if this world were everything.

And sometimes we forget that we are also wealthy in blessings already received and in present opportunity to commune with God. Think of it—God "has blessed us in the heavenly realms with every spiritual blessing in Christ" (Eph. 1:3), and he desires a warm, personal relationship with every believer!

Fellow Christians, let's wake up and enter into our great inheritance. Let us glorify and enjoy the Father, Son, and Holy Spirit now and forever.

Review Questions

1. Does Jesus teach in John 15:22-25 that the Jewish leaders were not guilty before they heard his messages and saw his signs? Explain.

2. Show how God used the selfish actions of the soldiers in John 19:23-24 to fulfill an Old Testament prediction.

3. Since Jesus had not yet come, how were Old Testament believers saved?

4. What is meant by the "already" and the "not yet"?

5. Is there a sense in which even the second coming and believers' glorification are already fulfilled? Explain.

Discussion Questions

1. Make a study of Old Testament passages fulfilled in the Gospel of John.

2. Why from a biblical standpoint is our time the most exciting in the history of the world?

3. How do you explain the thanklessness of the average person today? How can we as God's people become more thankful to him and to others?

4. Are you able to fit together salvation by grace and judgment based on works?

5. Show how an understanding of the tension between the "already" and the "not yet" can help us better cope with the death of a beloved Christian, a chronic illness, and other hardships.

Index of Scripture

Index of Topics